UNLESS YOU
TAKE UP YOUR CROSS

Lenten Reflection and Devotion

Robert D. Eimer, O.M.l.
Sarah O'Malley, O.S.B.

A Liturgical Press Book

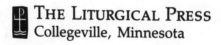 THE LITURGICAL PRESS
Collegeville, Minnesota

Cover design by Ann Blattner
Cover photos by Bill Magrath
Icons in photos by Sr. Mary Charles McGough, O.S.B.

1   2   3   4   5   6   7   8   9

Library of Congress Cataloging-in-Publication Data

Eimer, Robert, 1927-
   Unless you take up your cross : a daily Lenten devotional / Robert
D. Eimer, Sarah A. O'Malley.
      p.   cm.
   ISBN 0-8146-2063-9
   1. Lent—Prayer-books and devotions—English. 2. Holy Cross-
-Prayer-books and devotions—English.   I. O'Malley, Sarah.
II. Title.
BX2170.L4E33   1991
242'.34—dc20   91-40223
                                                          CIP

DEDICATION

*Dedicated to our sisters and brothers
who have encouraged and
supported us in countless ways.*

CONTENTS

INTRODUCTION

Unless You Take Up Your Cross is meant to be a companion for any individual (or group) looking for a devotional for Lent. Each day, this devotional presents a Christian value, mystery or virtue associated with the cross. At the heart of each devotion is the cross, which is used ritually to begin and end the service of the day.

Although the devotions are designed principally for the individual, they are easily adaptable for groups, such as support groups and Bible study groups. The reflections can also be used as prayer services for RCIA, staff, and parish council meetings.

The format is as follows: the individual is invited to take the cross in hand and sign himself/herself. A familiar antiphon follows, then a brief passage from Scripture, a reflection on the passage, and thought provoking questions. As a result of the reflection on Scripture, an action is suggested. The suggested action is just that—suggested. It is not meant to burden the individual with forty-seven additional tasks during Lent. With due respect for personal initiative and freedom, let the Holy Spirit be the mover to action. As regards the four petitions that follow the suggested action, a distinction is made between personal prayer and a ministry of prayer that stretches the individual to pray for the needs of the larger world community. The last of the four petitions is for personal needs and self-growth. Finally, a concluding prayer and a ritual veneration of the cross bring the devotion to an end. Kissing the cross symbolizes our love for the crucified Savior.

The daily devotion can be completed comfortably in about ten minutes. This allows even a busy person the time needed for a thoughtful reading of the Word of God, the Personal Application and the Reflective Questions. A period of silence after the

Personal Application and Reflective Questions would be appropriate. Obviously, a quiet setting and a burning candle placed near the cross would enhance the prayer space.

Though at times this devotional may correspond closely to the daily Lenten readings, it is not designed around the Lectionary. The cross is the unifying focus of each day. The Scripture chosen relates to the varied Christian values, mysteries, or virtues seen in the light of the cross.

We wish to thank Rose Eilering for her typing. Her patience will not be forgotten. Likewise, we also thank Barbara Kaiser, Mary Kay Way, and June Bricker for their typing skills. We give special thanks to Sr. Lucille Geisinger, O.S.B., for her meticulous work in proofreading and typing the manuscript.

The cover design features the artwork of Sr. Mary Charles McGough, O.S.B. The icon was commissioned by The Oblates of Mary Immaculate as part of the processional cross for the new church at The Shrine of Our Lady of the Snows, Belleville, Illinois.

ASH WEDNESDAY

A cross should be visible and may be used to sign oneself as follows: In the name of the Father, Son, and Holy Spirit. Amen.

OPENING ANTIPHON

I adore you, O Christ, and I praise you because by your holy cross you have redeemed the world.

THE CROSS AND CONVERSION
WORD OF GOD

Yet even now, says the LORD, return to me with your whole heart, with fasting, and weeping, and mourning; rend your hearts, not your garments, and return to the LORD, your God (Joel 2:12-13).

PERSONAL APPLICATION

Acting as God's messenger, the prophet Joel calls Israel to repent in the face of an impending disaster—an invasion of locusts. Although circumstances vary, the call to repentance is found in both the Old and New Testaments. On Ash Wednesday, the Church adopts this reading to call the people of God and each individual to a whole-hearted conversion to Christ and his ideals. Thus Lent goes far beyond the externals of fast and abstinence, and focuses on an internal change of heart.

The essential conversion is to Christ: allowing him to become the center of our hearts, our lives, and our decisions. Placing Christ in the center demands a renewed commitment to Gospel

9

values—such as growing in reverence for life and working for justice for all peoples.

What a task it is to shape our behavior according to the Gospel ideals of Jesus—following the command to love God with our whole heart, our whole mind, and our whole self, and our neighbor as ourself. That means moving well beyond the observance of the Ten Commandments, to embrace the Beatitudes.

Conversion also demands reshaping our attitudes towards the Church, perhaps becoming a more active participant in the Church's worship or getting involved in the work and mission of the Church.

Such a conversion—to Jesus, his ideals, and the Church—takes a lifetime. The invitation of Joel, "Return to me with your whole heart," is repeated until the day we die.

Reflective Questions:

1) Jesus calls us to friendship with him. How would I describe my relationship with him?
2) What areas of my heart still need conversion?

Suggested Action:

Read the passage from John 15:13-15 and reflect on the quality of your friendship with Christ.

MINISTRY OF PRAYER

For conversion of the Church to Gospel ideals . . . Lord, hear my prayer.

For alienated Catholics and those who have not yet encountered Christ . . . Lord, hear my prayer.

For conversion in our lives and the lives of our families . . . Lord, hear my prayer.

For a deeper awareness of the areas of my life that need conversion . . . Lord, hear my prayer.

CONCLUDING PRAYER

Heavenly Father, I begin this Lent with a sign of death—the marking of my forehead with ashes. Let it be the death of my old self and the beginning of the new. Send your amazing grace to open my heart to Jesus and to live more deeply in his love. Help me to continue my conversion to Gospel ideals and to deepen my participation in the life of the Church. Amen.

(In conclusion, you are invited to take up the cross and kiss it.)

✝

THURSDAY AFTER ASH WEDNESDAY

A cross should be visible and may be used to sign oneself as follows: In the name of the Father, Son, and Holy Spirit. Amen.

OPENING ANTIPHON

Christ has died, Christ is risen, Christ will come again.

THE CROSS AND ALMSGIVING
WORD OF GOD

But when you give alms, do not let your left hand know what your right is doing, so that your almsgiving may be secret. And your Father who sees in secret will repay you (Matt 6:3-4).

PERSONAL APPLICATION

For the pious Jew of old, almsgiving was a venerated practice and a pillar of his/her spiritual life. But, in a Christian context, almsgiving takes on a deeper meaning for God's people. First, the giving of alms reflects the Father's generous love shown in the crucifixion and death of his only Son who gave his life for our sake. Second, it reflects our faith—a faith that sees Jesus in the hungry, the naked, the persecuted, the homeless. What a sorry motive it is to give alms out of a desire for praise or public recognition. Such is the gist of the admonition from Matthew, quoted above.

The world today is burdened with abject poverty that can be alleviated by our almsgiving. Whether we contribute to the Catholic Relief Services in aiding Third World countries, or to the Campaign for Human Development, a self-help program for the poor; to diocesan charities or the local food shelf; to the St. Vincent de Paul Society or to those who shelter the homeless, we minister to Jesus who identifies with the poor and needy.

Lent is an appropriate time to examine our budgets and to find ways to contribute to organizations that have proven records of alleviating poverty. However, the challenge of our Lenten almsgiving does not end with our budgets. Our giving must also be connected with the self-denial inspired by the cross. In giving up food by our fasting or denying ourselves legitimate pleasures, our almsgiving becomes blessed because of its personal cost. Finally, it is in such sacrificial giving that we experience the hunger and deprivation of the poor.

Reflective Questions:

1) How is the value of almsgiving expressed in my life?
2) How does my budget reflect my Gospel values?

Suggested Action:

On the basis of your budget, decide what amount you can give to charity during Lent.

MINISTRY OF PRAYER

For the many charitable organizations that reach out to the poor . . . Lord, hear my prayer.

For Christians, that they may find unpretentious ways to support worthy charities . . . Lord, hear my prayer.

For continuing cooperation among Christian denominations to meet the needs of the poor . . . Lord, hear my prayer.

That the Spirit enable me to discern how to assist needy people when I personally encounter them . . . Lord, hear my prayer.

CONCLUDING PRAYER

Jesus, guide me to discover ways to personally sacrifice so as to share with those who are hungry, abandoned, homeless, and in need of clothing. Purify my faith so that my prime motive in giving will be love for you rather than need for praise or public recognition. Amen.

(In conclusion, you are invited to take up the cross and kiss it.)

✝

FRIDAY AFTER ASH WEDNESDAY

A cross should be visible and may be used to sign oneself as follows: In the name of the Father, Son, and Holy Spirit. Amen.

OPENING ANTIPHON

Dying you destroyed our death; rising you restored our life. Lord Jesus, come in glory.

THE CROSS AND PRAYER
WORD OF GOD

When you pray, do not be like the hypocrites, who love to stand and pray in the synagogues and on street corners so that others may see them. Amen, I say to you, they have received their reward. But when you pray, go to your inner room, close the door, and pray to your Father in secret. . . . In praying, do not babble like pagans, who think that they will be heard because of their many words (Matt 6:5-7).

PERSONAL APPLICATION

It's clear that Jesus' warning refers more to motivation for prayer than to the form of prayer. Like any other conscientious

Jew, Jesus prayed both in the synagogues and in private. The point that he makes is that all prayer, public or private, is meant to praise God and not ourselves.

Jesus nourished his life of prayer by retreating to lonely places in order to pray privately. On such occasions, Jesus may have simply praised his Father, or asked for the wisdom to choose his twelve apostles, or prayed for the strength to accept his Father's will by taking up the cross.

Before all else, to pray is to become aware of God's presence within and around us. Even when using a prayerbook or rosary, it is important that we take some quiet time to allow the heart to center on God's presence before beginning the vocal prayer.

During Lent we are challenged to reflect on the motive and style of our personal prayer. Where is the quiet space in our busy lives, the space that invites us to personalize God's overwhelming love for us, his people?

Likewise, we are challenged to accept God's will in our lives. No matter what our request might be, no matter how holy it is, we implicitly pray that God's will be done. Sometimes we know, as Jesus did in the Garden of Gethsemane, that God's will means bearing the cross. Like Jesus, who received an angel of comfort, we ask the Father to give us the peace and strength to accept our cross.

Reflective Questions:

1) How do I experience God's will directing my life?
2) How is my prayer life influencing the rest of my daily life?

Suggested Action:

Pray earnestly for someone in your neighborhood who is suffering from sickness or any other cross.

MINISTRY OF PRAYER

For a growing awareness of God's presence in Scripture, world events, nature, other people, and in myself . . . Lord, hear my prayer.

14

For Sunday worship in my parish, that it will become more dynamic . . . Lord, hear my prayer.

For parents, that they will help their children develop a life of personal prayer . . . Lord, hear my prayer.

For greater acceptance of God's will in my life . . . Lord, hear my prayer.

CONCLUDING PRAYER

Jesus, I know that prayer is like breathing in your life, love, and strength, and breathing out my praise, love, and thanks to you. Be with me in my struggle to accept the Father's will, especially when it means carrying the cross in my life. Give me the strength and peace to say, like you, "Father, not my will but yours be done." Amen.

(In conclusion, you are invited to take up the cross and kiss it.)

SATURDAY AFTER ASH WEDNESDAY

A cross should be visible and may be used to sign oneself as follows: In the name of the Father, Son, and Holy Spirit. Amen.

OPENING ANTIPHON

Lord, by your cross and resurrection, you have set us free. You are the Savior of the world.

THE CROSS AND FASTING
WORD OF GOD

When you fast, do not look gloomy like the hypocrites. They neglect their appearance so that they may appear to others to be fasting. . . . anoint your head and wash your face, so that you may not appear to be fasting, except to your Father who is hidden. And your Father who sees what is hidden will repay you (Matt 6:16-18).

PERSONAL APPLICATION

In Jesus' time, pious people like the Pharisees fasted twice a week. They fasted for various reasons: purifying themselves, making their prayers effective, and humbling their hearts before God. No matter what the reason for fasting, Jesus points out the danger of spiritual pride if one fasts in order to be seen by others.

Although the Pharisees accused Jesus of discouraging fasting among his disciples, he did not actually condemn the practice. What he did say was that his disciples would fast once he, the Bridegroom, had departed. After Jesus had ascended into heaven, the Church again encouraged the practice of fasting, especially on certain days during Lent.

The twentieth-century Church advocates fasting, but not in morbid excess. Fasting for forty days is not mandated, but some form of self-denial throughout Lent is still encouraged: for example, denying ourselves coffee, sweets, liquor, or cigarettes. Although fasting, in a way, is a participation in the cross of Jesus (we crucify our desires as Paul says) the Church no longer emphasizes fasting as a way of disciplining the body. Instead, the Church urges us—through soup suppers and food drives—to take the money saved from fasting and use it to help the poor. To the extent that we say "no" to our bodily desires out of love for God and neighbor, self-denial truly becomes a religious act and, in a spiritual way, participates in Christ's cross. Fasting is done not in order to be seen but rather to help others.

Reflective Questions:

1) Is self-discipline of my body the main reason for my fasting?
2) Do I make a practical connection between fasting and helping the poor? How does my fasting benefit the needy?

Suggested Action:

Choose one concrete practice of self-denial that will benefit both you and the needy.

MINISTRY OF PRAYER

For the spirit of fasting in the Church leading to a greater love of God and our neighbor . . . Lord, hear my prayer.

For cheerfulness in serving the Lord even when it involves self-denial and fasting . . . Lord, hear my prayer.

For those afflicted by eating disorders of any kind . . . Lord, hear my prayer.

For the grace needed to be faithful to my Lenten practice of self-denial . . . Lord, hear my prayer.

CONCLUDING PRAYER

Heavenly Father, strengthen me with the discipline of fasting, not so much to make me strong-willed as to make me generous to those in need. Let me choose to deny myself so that I might reach out to those who are hungry and poor. I ask this through Christ our Lord. Amen.

(In conclusion, you are invited to take up the cross and kiss it.)

FIRST SUNDAY OF LENT

A cross should be visible and may be used to sign oneself as follows: In the name of the Father, Son, and Holy Spirit. Amen.

OPENING ANTIPHON

Christ became obedient for us, even to death, dying on the cross.

THE CROSS AND TEMPTATION
WORD OF GOD

At once the Spirit drove him out into the desert, and he remained in the desert for forty days, tempted by Satan. He was among wild beasts, and the angels ministered to him (Mark 1:12-13).

PERSONAL APPLICATION

Just as Moses and the Israelites experienced forty years of desert life, Jesus, as the new Moses, was led by the Spirit into a desert experience of forty days. There he confronted Satan's temptations and made important decisions about his future public life.

Matthew and Luke describe in more detail than Mark the three-fold temptations which center on the misuse of spiritual power. As one spiritual giant encountering another, Satan realizes that Jesus has immense spiritual power. Satan is willing to make Jesus the human king of his worldly empire if he but pledge allegiance to demonic power. Jesus rejects Satan and the temptations to worldly glory and power and chooses rather to serve the needs of people.

We are all faced with similar temptations and choices. Our consumer society daily bombards us through the media with the message that life should be pain-free and joy-filled in our pursuit of creature comforts. The world tempts us to compromise our Christian values in business, politics and the social arena. In some Latin American countries, Christians have become martyrs for the sake of justice and human dignity. In the United States, it takes the "stuff of martyrs" to remain true to Gospel values. To resist the easy, comfortable way, to hold firm to our integrity in difficult situations leads us to another way—the way of the cross.

Reflective Questions:

1) What are the main temptations I encounter in my work and in my neighborhood?
2) How are my good works an extension of Christ's giving on the cross?

Suggested Action:

Read Matthew's account of the temptation scene (Matt 4:1-11) and reflect on it in light of your own present struggles.

MINISTRY OF PRAYER

For all in Church leadership, that they may see their ministry as one of service, not of power . . . Lord, hear my prayer.

For those severely tempted by drugs, money, power, or fame . . . Lord, hear my prayer.

That God may strengthen parents to sacrifice for their families . . . Lord, hear my prayer.

For the light to see and use my talents in service to the Church . . . Lord, hear my prayer.

CONCLUDING PRAYER

Jesus, you were tempted as I am. As I face the daily temptations of my world, walk with me and inspire me to see beyond the false claims and empty promises of Satan. May the cross remind me of your selfless gift of love. Amen.

(In conclusion, you are invited to take up the cross and kiss it.)

MONDAY IN FIRST WEEK OF LENT

A cross should be visible and may be used to sign oneself as follows: In the name of the Father, Son, and Holy Spirit. Amen.

OPENING ANTIPHON

Those who sow in tears shall reap with shouts of joy.

THE CROSS AND JOURNEY
WORD OF GOD

Then he said to all, "If anyone wishes to come after me, he must deny himself and take up his cross daily and follow me" (Luke 9:23).

PERSONAL APPLICATION

Only Luke, of all the evangelists, adds the word "daily" to Jesus' invitation to discipleship. By the time Luke wrote his Gospel, the focus was more on the daily demands of Christian living than on imminent martyrdom.

The journey we are invited to take may include failure to live up to the ideals of discipleship or reluctance to carry the cross when we feel tired, discouraged, or hurt. Like Peter, we may deny Jesus when faced with danger or ridicule, or even betray him, as Judas did, for money.

The trouble with life is that it's so daily. The grind, the boredom, the fatigue, the clash of personalities in the working place, the struggle with traffic, the noise—all these make up part of the "terrible daily routine."

The journey doesn't get easier when we face old age. Only when we've experienced arthritis, or sleeplessness, cataracts or faltering steps or hearing loss do we realize that the cross remains a challenging part of our journey until our last breath.

No one need walk the path alone. Jesus has promised to walk at our side, and our brothers and sisters in the Church will be there for us when we need their help. Finally, those who have journeyed before us will be with us in our sojourn and make powerful intercession for us.

Reflective Questions:

1) Where do I experience the daily cross in my life?
2) Who has been a support to me in my times of darkness?

Suggested Action:

Imagine the Lord walking beside you. Share with him your struggles, whatever they may be: work, health, grief.

MINISTRY OF PRAYER

For those who carry a cross of persecution and misunderstanding . . . Lord, hear my prayer.

For those struggling with poverty . . . Lord, hear my prayer.

For those who bear a cross of illness . . . Lord, hear my prayer.

That I may not grow weary of carrying my daily cross . . .
Lord, hear my prayer.

CONCLUDING PRAYER

Lord of the journey, my temptation is to lay down the burden and seek a world without the cross. To journey with you is to carry the cross made for my shoulders. Strengthen me so that I can accept the difficult duties and frustrations that face me each day. I ask this in your name. Amen.

(In conclusion, you are invited to take up the cross and kiss it.)

TUESDAY IN FIRST WEEK OF LENT

A cross should be visible and may be used to sign oneself as follows: In the name of the Father, Son, and Holy Spirit. Amen.

OPENING ANTIPHON

Blessed be the Lord day after day, the God who saves us and bears our burdens.

THE CROSS AND DEATH
WORD OF GOD

Jesus answered them, "The hour has come for the Son of Man to be glorified. Amen, amen, I say to you, unless a grain of wheat falls to the ground and dies, it remains just a grain of wheat; but if it dies, it produces much fruit" (John 12:23-24).

PERSONAL APPLICATION

In John's Gospel, Jesus used an earthy example to illustrate a profound mystery: how death can lead to new life. However,

21

Jesus' death led not only to new life for himself but also for all humankind. He became the Savior of the world.

Jesus accepted his Father's plan, which included the cross and death as his ultimate act of obedience—"Father, into your hands I commend my spirit" (Luke 23:46).

Not many of us can welcome death like St. Francis of Assisi, who prayed, "Come, Sister Death." However, we grow in our acceptance of God's will by accepting our many daily crosses and thus prepare for the final act of resignation: saying "yes" to God at the time of our death.

Letting go of those we love, surrendering our very life is the supreme task facing all human beings. Likewise for followers of Christ, it is our greatest challenge. Only through trust in a God who loves us and prepares a place for us are we able to follow Christ, who conquered death once and for all.

In the eyes of faith, death is the gateway to new life, a life that exceeds our wildest dreams. Our American society, which sees death as a wall, and not a door, simply denies the reality of death and the redemptive value of suffering. As Christians, we bear witness to the meaning of death because we believe that death is the entrance to a greater life.

Reflective Questions:

    1) Where in my daily life is God inviting me to let go of some person or thing?

    2) At this moment in my life, how do I imagine my death? What words come to mind in describing it? Fear, joy, pain, anger, abandonment?

Suggested Action:

Visit, telephone, or send a card to someone who is grieving the death of a loved one.

MINISTRY OF PRAYER

For all those in my parish who will die in the coming year . . . Lord, hear my prayer.

For all who are suffering because of cancer, AIDS, or other diseases . . . Lord, hear my prayer.

That God strengthen those who minister to adolescents engaged in a life/death struggle with addictions or violence . . . Lord, hear my prayer.

That by facing my death honestly, I may learn to treasure each day to its full . . . Lord, hear my prayer.

CONCLUDING PRAYER

Creator God, your Son, Jesus, accepted the mystery of death with faith and hope. Comfort me in my final hour and give me that same faith and hope. May Jesus, Mary, and Joseph be with me now and at the hour of my death. Amen.

(In conclusion, you are invited to take up the cross and kiss it.)

WEDNESDAY IN FIRST WEEK OF LENT

A cross should be visible and may be used to sign oneself as follows: In the name of the Father, Son, and Holy Spirit. Amen.

OPENING ANTIPHON

God did not spare his Son, but gave him up to suffer for our sake.

THE CROSS AND SERVICE
WORD OF GOD

. . . he [Jesus] rose from supper and took off his outer garments. He took a towel and tied it around his waist. Then he poured water into a basin and began to wash the disciples' feet and dry them with the towel around his waist (John 13:4-5).

PERSONAL APPLICATION

In the narrative of the Last Supper, John's account is unique. Rather than a simple retelling of the words of consecration, John concentrates on the meaning of that event for the Church. By relating the washing of feet, he dramatizes the relationship between Eucharist and service. As Jesus said, "I have given you a model to follow, so that as I have done for you, you should also do" (John 13:15).

How shocking it was to Jesus' followers to see him die the horrible death reserved by Romans for criminals or rebellious, runaway slaves! However, in washing feet Jesus had already taken on the role of a slave, since slaves generally performed that menial task.

In our lives Eucharist is not only the peak of our worship experience but also the fountain of Christian ministry. The connection between the sacrifice of the cross and service to others has continued down the ages in the Mass. As Jesus gave himself on the cross out of love for us, so the disciples are asked to serve others in imitation of his love.

Vatican Council II opened the door to many new ministries for lay people. Jesus continues to serve the world through us, using our voices, hands and feet, gifts and talents. Lent challenges all of us to discover new ways to serve.

Reflective Questions:

1) How does the celebration of the Eucharist move me to serve others?
2) Which person/persons do I find difficult to serve? Can I see these people in the light of the cross?

Suggested Action:

Reflect on a talent or gift you have received from God. Volunteer to use it in service of others.

MINISTRY OF PRAYER

For the Pope, that he may become the servant of the servants of God . . . Lord, hear my prayer.

For our bishops and clergy, that they may share with us the ministry of leadership . . . Lord, hear my prayer.

For all men and women, religious and lay, that they may use their gifts for others . . . Lord, hear my prayer.

That through a deeper faith I may see Christ in those I serve, even the difficult ones . . . Lord, hear my prayer.

CONCLUDING PRAYER

Jesus, in your public ministry you served all you met, becoming a "person for others." By your cross, you gave us the ultimate service by offering your life to redeem us from the slavery of sin. Grant me the grace to recognize my talents and to use them in ministry to others, thus becoming a "person for others." Amen.

(In conclusion, you are invited to take up the cross and kiss it.)

THURSDAY IN FIRST WEEK OF LENT

A cross should be visible and may be used to sign oneself as follows: In the name of the Father, Son, and Holy Spirit. Amen.

OPENING ANTIPHON

Through his suffering, my servant shall justify many, and their guilt he shall bear.

THE CROSS AND DISCIPLESHIP
WORD OF GOD

For whoever wishes to save his life will lose it, but whoever loses his life for my sake and that of the Gospel will save it (Mark 8:35).

PERSONAL APPLICATION

A disciple is known as one who freely puts himself/herself at the feet of the Master to embrace his views and teachings. In the Old Testament, prophets and rabbis had their disciples. Discipleship in early times emphasized the personal authority of the teacher and the passing on of tradition from the teacher to the disciple. In the New Testament, John the Baptist, a contemporary of Jesus, had his disciples, some of whom later became followers of Jesus.

Jesus had unique requirements for his disciples. Jesus called his disciples, not on the basis of their intellectual abilities, but on the basis of their personal attachment to him and his message. His "Follow me" is a call to break with the past or even one's own family in order to be free to fashion one's life after his. Christian disciples are bound primarily to a person— Jesus. To follow him means to share in his cross, his ideals, and eventually his kingdom.

Down through the ages, Jesus continues to challenge us to be his disciples and to be countercultural by going against worldly values. We avoid "consumerism" or a compulsion to accumulate things, because Christ calls for simplicity. We seek "peace" and struggle to help the poor because Christ gave us these ideals. If we truly live the Gospel, we will soon be carrying our cross. What they did to the teacher, they will do to the disciple.

Reflective Questions:

1) In baptism and confirmation, Jesus has called me to be his disciple. Now, as an adult, what is one area where I need to resist a false value in my culture?
2) How do I strengthen my bond of discipleship? By reading Scripture? Through personal prayer? By frequent Eucharist?

Suggested Action:

Read Luke 6:13-49 for one description of discipleship. Reflect on its message.

MINISTRY OF PRAYER

That less committed Christians may become strong, active disciples of Jesus . . . Lord, hear my prayer.

For the strength to follow Jesus despite the cross . . . Lord, hear my prayer.

For those persecuted because of their commitment to Christ and his ideals . . . Lord, hear my prayer.

That my commitment to Jesus may become deeper and more loving . . . Lord, hear my prayer.

CONCLUDING PRAYER

Jesus, through baptism, I became part of your Christian family. Now, as an adult, I consciously choose you as the Lord of my life and the way to the Father. Strengthen me as your disciple, especially in moments of suffering and doubt. Inspire me to imitate Mary, who whole-heartedly became your first disciple. Amen.

(In conclusion, you are invited to take up the cross and kiss it.)

FRIDAY IN FIRST WEEK OF LENT

A cross should be visible and may be used to sign oneself as follows: In the name of the Father, Son, and Holy Spirit. Amen.

OPENING ANTIPHON

Christ had to suffer and rise from the dead, and so enter into his glory.

THE CROSS AND MYSTERY
WORD OF GOD

Oh, the depth of the riches and wisdom and knowledge of God! How inscrutable are his judgments and how unsearchable his ways! "For who has known the mind of the Lord or who has been his counselor?" (Rom 11:33-34).

PERSONAL APPLICATION

A crucified god was repulsive to the minds of Greek philosophers and a scandal in the eyes of the Jews. How could an all-powerful God allow people to treat his Son in such a way? Paul's answer to the crucifixion is found in his First Letter to the Corinthians: according to God's plan for all ages, the cross is a mystery to be accepted in faith.

Part of the mystery concerns human freedom and the suffering that results from sin. It was not God the Father who crucified Jesus but the Romans at the instigation of some Jewish leaders. The mystery is that God not only allows human freedom but also its abuse. What is more, God can bring good out of evil as is evidenced in the redemption which came forth from the crucifixion of Jesus.

Another aspect of the mystery of the cross is the suffering Jesus endured. His suffering raises questions about the manifold suffering in our world. Why must innocent people suffer? Why is life taken away at an early age? How can a loving God allow so much violence and abuse?

The cross remains a mystery as does God's plan for each of us. Most questions about suffering will not be answered here, but in the hereafter. For now, we are left with faith.

Reflective Questions:

1) Have I experienced suffering because of other people's words and actions? Can I forgive them?
2) Where do I see the mystery of the cross manifested in my life?

Suggested Action:

Ponder the Serenity Prayer: God, grant me the serenity to accept the things I cannot change, courage to change the things I can, and wisdom to know the difference.

MINISTRY OF PRAYER

For those in the healing professions, that they continue to alleviate suffering . . . Lord, hear my prayer.

That people confronted by the mystery of the cross might be given the light of faith . . . Lord, hear my prayer.

For the wisdom to discern when suffering is redemptive or of our own making . . . Lord, hear my prayer.

For greater acceptance of the mystery of suffering in my life . . . Lord, hear my prayer.

CONCLUDING PRAYER

Lord, each day I encounter the mystery of the cross as it shadows my life and my world. You challenge me to alleviate the sufferings of others whenever possible. Give me the faith to accept the mystery of the cross and to believe that through my suffering will come salvation. Amen.

(In conclusion, you are invited to take up the cross and kiss it.)

SATURDAY IN FIRST WEEK OF LENT

A cross should be visible and may be used to sign oneself as follows: In the name of the Father, Son, and Holy Spirit. Amen.

OPENING ANTIPHON

I adore you, O Christ, and I praise you because by your cross you have redeemed the world.

THE CROSS AND COURAGE
WORD OF GOD

Can you drink the cup that I drink or be baptized with the baptism with which I am baptized? (Mark 10:38).

PERSONAL APPLICATION

After the disciples James and John had asked Jesus if they could sit at his right and left when he came into his glory, Jesus countered with this question: "Can you drink the cup that I drink?"—that is, do you have the courage to share in the suffering I will undergo? In an eager but naive way, they replied, "We can." How quickly their courage vanished when at Golgotha they deserted their master. Only later, after the resurrection, would they share in the cup of suffering or know the price of discipleship.

Each Mass reminds us of Jesus' question: "Can you drink the cup I drink?" Courage does not mean a lack of fear; Jesus himself experienced fear in the Garden of Gethsemane. Courage does not mean seeking the cross as a good in itself, for Jesus begged the Father to rid him of the cross if possible. Courage means being faithful to the Gospel message of love and justice even in the face of persecution.

We are not usually asked to be martyrs for the faith, but we are asked to carry a daily cross. Some saints refer to this cross as "the tedious daily death."

What in our lives today demands courage? To take an ethical but unpopular stance in the marketplace, politics, and social settings is truly courageous. To stand up for a consistent life ethic from womb to tomb is to know firsthand what courage can cost. As St. John Vianney said, "You must accept your cross; if you carry it courageously, it will carry you to heaven."

Reflective Questions:

1) In what specific area of my life is Jesus calling me to act in a courageous way?
2) In the face of pain and persecution, do I have any special prayer/devotion that gives me strength to carry on?

Suggested Action:

Remember a time when God gave you the strength and courage to face a difficulty or trial. Thank the Lord in the quiet of your heart.

MINISTRY OF PRAYER

That Christians be given courage to act on their convictions . . . Lord, hear my prayer.

For people who face terminal illness, that God may give them peace and strength . . . Lord, hear my prayer.

For the wisdom to find ways to bring Christian values to the political and business world . . . Lord, hear my prayer.

For the days I need courage to get up in the morning and face my daily tasks . . . Lord, hear my prayer.

CONCLUDING PRAYER

Jesus, my strength, in my daily life you ask me to drink from the cup of suffering. May I use the special graces of this Lenten season to deepen my love for you. Grant me the strength to accept the crosses of everyday living, and, in the end, give me the courage to face my own death with hope and faith. Amen.

(In conclusion, you are invited to take up the cross and kiss it.)

SECOND SUNDAY OF LENT

A cross should be visible and may be used to sign oneself as follows: In the name of the Father, Son, and Holy Spirit. Amen.

OPENING ANTIPHON

Christ has died, Christ is risen, Christ will come again.

THE CROSS AND PURIFICATION
WORD OF GOD

When he [prodigal son] had freely spent everything, a severe famine struck that country, and he found himself in dire need. So he hired himself out to one of the local citizens who sent him to his farm to tend the swine. And he longed to eat his fill of the pods on which the swine fed, but nobody gave him any. Coming to his senses he thought, "How many of my father's hired workers have more than enough food to eat, but here am I, dying from hunger. I shall get up and go to my father and I shall say to him,

'Father, I have sinned against heaven and against you. I no longer deserve to be called your son . . . ' " (Luke 15:14-18).

PERSONAL APPLICATION

The cross can be a source of purification, even when it's of our own making. That is the meaning of the parable of the prodigal son. After wasting his inheritance, the errant son felt, for the first time, the suffering of poverty, rejection, and loneliness. An inexperienced, arrogant youth, he hadn't realized the goodness of his father until he personally encountered hunger, humiliation and suffering. Then, in a moment of grace, he decided to return to the father, purified—that is, more humble, more grateful and probably more compassionate.

Sometimes we create our own crosses. God allows us to "mess up," knowing that the consequences can help us grow. In the parable, the father didn't want his son to suffer; yet he didn't rescue his son. Today such parental action is called "tough love." The cross of hunger became a catalyst to purify the son of his self-centeredness and ingratitude.

Purification! How painful for all of us! However, to the degree that we say "yes" to God's grace, we can move from bitterness to blessing; from despair to hope. Both criminals crucified with Jesus turned to him: one to curse Jesus; another, Dismas, to receive his blessing.

In a sense, we are all prodigal daughters and sons of a compassionate Father who allows us to stumble and fall in order that we might learn from our failures. Sometimes only the pangs of hunger will draw us back to God.

Reflective Questions:

    1) In what ways have certain failures helped me to become a better person?
    2) What crisis created in me a deeper need for God?

Suggested Action:

Read Luke 15:11-32 and visualize yourself as the prodigal son or daughter.

MINISTRY OF PRAYER

For those who have wandered far from the Lord, that the pangs of hunger lead them back to the Father . . . Lord, hear my prayer.

That people struggling with depression may find new hope in God . . . Lord, hear my prayer.

For individuals who suffer from self-made crosses . . . Lord, hear my prayer.

That God may cleanse me of hidden pride and stubborn willfulness . . . Lord, hear my prayer.

CONCLUDING PRAYER

O Lord, the cross has the power to purify by freeing me from self-centeredness, arrogance, and self-indulgence. While never seeking the cross, enable me to accept the crosses that life imposes, and help me to learn from them the lessons of humility and compassion. Amen.

(In conclusion, you are invited to take up the cross and kiss it.)

MONDAY IN SECOND WEEK OF LENT

A cross should be visible and may be used to sign oneself as follows: In the name of the Father, Son, and Holy Spirit. Amen.

OPENING ANTIPHON

Dying you destroyed our death, rising you restored our life. Lord Jesus, come in glory.

THE CROSS AND LONG-SUFFERING
WORD OF GOD

But we hold this treasure in earthen vessels, that the surpassing power may be of God and not from us. We are afflicted in every way, but not constrained; perplexed, but not driven to despair; persecuted, but not abandoned; struck down, but not destroyed; always carrying about in the body the dying of Jesus, so that the life of Jesus may also be manifested in our body (2 Cor 4:7-10).

PERSONAL APPLICATION

In this passage, Paul describes not only endurance in the face of the cross but also faith-filled patience and steadfastness. He is afflicted in multiple ways but never gives up his trust in God.

We may wonder at times how we would respond if confronted with death by martyrdom. What may be even more difficult than martyrdom is the day-by-day protracted struggle to live our faith in the face of opposition or in the shadow of suffering. To remain constant and strong in oppressive situations demands heroic perseverance, sometimes referred to as long-suffering.

What situations might call for the virtue of long-suffering? Ridicule by fellow workers, daily criticism of one's faith, long standing physical or emotional ills, caring for a life-long invalid are practical examples.

A caution: long-suffering is not the endurance of evils that could be eliminated. For example, a woman shouldn't endure abuse from a violent husband for the sake of Christ. Such evil needs to be confronted, not passively accepted.

Long-suffering, the power to hold on to faith and hope while enduring, comes from the cross. It is a special grace that only Christ can give us. Like Paul, we bear the cross in our body so that the life of Jesus may also be manifested in our body.

Reflective Questions:

1) Who is my present-day model of long-suffering?
2) Have I at times been passive rather than assertive in the face of evil?

Suggested Action:

Visit someone who has endured sickness for a long time to get a sense of what keeps him/her going.

MINISTRY OF PRAYER

That young Christians might be able to withstand the ridicule of peers . . . Lord, hear my prayer.

That those who must endure tedious and boring jobs may not get discouraged . . . Lord, hear my prayer.

For people with Alzheimer's disease or stroke . . . Lord, hear my prayer.

That I may have the courage to report abusive behavior when I experience or see it . . . Lord, hear my prayer.

CONCLUDING PRAYER

God of compassion, I am only an earthen vessel in need of your power to endure the many crosses in my life. Give me eyes of faith to look beyond my human frailty and brokenness to a new life in you. Amen.

(In conclusion, you are invited to take up the cross and kiss it.)

TUESDAY IN SECOND WEEK OF LENT

A cross should be visible and may be used to sign oneself as follows: In the name of the Father, Son, and Holy Spirit. Amen.

OPENING ANTIPHON

Lord, by your cross and resurrection you have set us free. You are the Savior of the world.

THE CROSS AND PRIESTHOOD
WORD OF GOD

While they were eating, he took bread, said the blessing, broke it, and gave it to them, and said, "Take it; this is my body."

Then he took a cup, gave thanks, and gave it to them, and they all drank from it. He said to them, "This is my blood of the covenant, which will be shed for many" (Mark 14:22-24).

PERSONAL APPLICATION

The Jewish Feast of Passover centered around a sacred meal which included lambs that had been sacrificed by their priests. The meal was a ritual remembrance, praising Yahweh for Israel's deliverance from Egyptian slavery.

The Last Supper, on Holy Thursday, was a celebration of the Passover. However, Jesus made a dramatic change in the ritual: he spoke about his own blood being shed for many. Instead of the lamb's blood saving the Israelites from the angel of death, Jesus became the lamb whose blood would save all of us.

By offering himself up for our sins, Jesus became both the Lamb of God and the presiding high priest. When Jesus asked that this new sacrifice be continued in memory of him, he transferred to his apostles the power to continue offering this sacrifice.

As Catholics, how fortunate we are to have a Eucharistic-centered spirituality. For us, the Mass is the heart of our community worship and unity. Even the homebound, by receiving Holy Communion on a regular weekly basis, are united with the worshiping community.

Finally, in the Vatican II vision of the Eucharist, the Mass is the powerhouse for and inspiration of all Christian ministry and good works. It is in ministering to others' needs that our own lives parallel that of Christ's—of being blessed, broken, and given to others.

Reflective Questions:

1) How do I prepare myself to participate in the Mass?
2) In what ways could I encourage my parish priest in his vocation?

Suggested Action:

Send a "Thank You" note or a letter of encouragement to your parish priest or remember him on his ordination date.

MINISTRY OF PRAYER

For an increase in vocations to the priesthood . . . Lord, hear my prayer.

For priests and deacons who are depressed, lonely, or confused . . . Lord, hear my prayer.

For a renewal of the Eucharist, that there may be a deeper understanding of its power and meaning . . . Lord, hear my prayer.

That I may develop a grateful heart through each Eucharist I celebrate . . . Lord, hear my prayer.

CONCLUDING PRAYER

God of Abraham, Isaac, and Jacob, you sent your Son as the great high priest. May the power of the symbols of bread and wine penetrate my heart so that the salvation begun on the cross may be confirmed in each Eucharist. Amen.

(In conclusion, you are invited to take up the cross and kiss it.)

WEDNESDAY IN SECOND WEEK OF LENT

A cross should be visible and may be used to sign oneself as follows: In the name of the Father, Son, and Holy Spirit. Amen.

OPENING ANTIPHON

Christ became obedient for us, even to death, dying on the cross.

THE CROSS AND SELF-DENIAL
WORD OF GOD

Whoever wishes to come after me must deny himself, take up his cross, and follow me (Mark 8:34).

PERSONAL APPLICATION

In this passage, Jesus is asking for a total commitment to himself that might lead to sacrificing life itself. However, Jesus is not asking that we destroy our personality. He wants us to develop a wholesome personality, a strong ego. In no way is he recruiting "wimps" or long-faced martyrs as his followers.

What Jesus is asking of his followers is a "no" to excessive ease and comfort; "no" to self-seeking; "no" to selfish desires. What Jesus is asking is a strong "yes" to himself. St. Richard of Chichester has written: "O most merciful Redeemer, Friend and Brother, may I know thee more clearly, love thee more dearly, and follow thee more nearly, forever and ever. Amen."

In our youth we may have given up candy and movies as our form of Lenten self-denial. If such actions were done out of love, the Lord looked kindly on them. But for the mature Christian in the post-Vatican II Church, self-denial is linked to service of our neighbor. For instance, in the Lenten practice of "soup suppers," we deny ourselves a big meal so that the money saved might be donated to the poor. Or, we may deny ourselves by giving some time and energy weekly to care for the homeless and hungry.

Where the Lord is, his servant will be. A servant is "for others." Jesus not only asks us to say "no" to our selfish desires, but he also asks us to serve others through our self-denial.

Reflective Questions:

1) Are my Lenten resolutions based on love for others?
2) Are there any community projects in which I can participate?

Suggested Action:

If you have not chosen a specific form of self-denial, choose one today.

MINISTRY OF PRAYER

For greater courage in following Jesus along the path of self-denial . . . Lord, hear my prayer.

For a selfless generosity in ministering to the poor . . . Lord, hear my prayer.

That with a joyful spirit Jesus may be known, loved, and followed . . . Lord, hear my prayer.

That my self-denial may be directed toward the service of others . . . Lord, hear my prayer.

CONCLUDING PRAYER

Ever loving God, it is so difficult to say "no" to my desires, my comfort, my pleasures. Guide me to find ways to be a selfless person, a person who gives to others of time, talent, and treasure. I ask this through Christ, who carried his cross and invites me to follow him. Amen.

(In conclusion, you are invited to take up the cross and kiss it.)

THURSDAY IN SECOND WEEK OF LENT

A cross should be visible and may be used to sign oneself as follows: In the name of the Father, Son, and Holy Spirit. Amen.

OPENING ANTIPHON

Those who sow in tears shall reap with shouts of joy.

THE CROSS AND RANSOM
WORD OF GOD

For the slave called in the Lord is a freed person in the Lord, just as the free person who has been called is a slave of Christ. You have been purchased at a price. Do not become slaves to human beings (1 Cor 7:22-23).

PERSONAL APPLICATION

Paul, in this passage to the Corinthians, proposes that all people have been freed because Christ, the generous master, has paid the price to purchase freedom for all. Using the language of Paul's age, we have become "Christ's property" and no longer belong to the world or to Satan.

In Paul's era, a slave became free by doing odd jobs and depositing the money in the temple of some god. After the slave had deposited his purchase price, he would, in the presence of his master and a priest, symbolically become the property of the god. That's what Paul had in mind when he wrote to the Corinthians that they had become slaves of Christ. However, unlike the temple transaction, it was not the slave who paid the price but Jesus.

What did our freedom cost? We were bought at a great price—literally "blood money." Jesus died that we might know the freedom of the children of God. We have been "redeemed" and have become precious in his eyes. Although Christ can lay claim to us, he respects our freedom, never forcing us to love him in return.

The freedom that Christ gives us is not automatic. Possible obstacles to human freedom are: inner fears and addictions, genetic factors and family of origin issues. The abundance of self-help groups in our society today highlights the role of other people in the process of growing into greater health and inner freedom. Growth groups, like Alcoholics Anonymous, while advocating the role of others, strongly affirm the need of God's grace.

Reflective Questions:

1) What am I willing to give Jesus in return for my freedom?
2) Have I really experienced the freedom of Christ? Or do I still feel trapped by fears and addictions?

Suggested Action:

Read Romans 8:28-39 and ponder the marvelous description of God's love.

MINISTRY OF PRAYER

That the love of Christ crucified will overcome any fear or anxiety in our lives . . . Lord, hear my prayer.

That the power of the Holy Week liturgy will touch the hearts of all Christians . . . Lord, hear my prayer.

That all may be free from the entrapment of addictions such as drugs, sex, food . . . Lord, hear my prayer.

That being ransomed by Christ, I may be free to serve others . . . Lord, hear my prayer.

CONCLUDING PRAYER

Lord, I can never realize your love for me until I understand the price you paid for my freedom and salvation. How precious, priceless is every human being in your loving eyes—the infant in the mother's womb, the addict, the person with AIDS, the disabled veteran. Grant freedom to your most abandoned children through the power of your cross. Amen.

(In conclusion, you are invited to take up the cross and kiss it.)

FRIDAY IN SECOND WEEK OF LENT

A cross should be visible and may be used to sign oneself as follows: In the name of the Father, Son, and Holy Spirit. Amen.

OPENING ANTIPHON

Blessed be the Lord, day after day, the God who saves us and bears our burdens.

THE CROSS AND FOLLY
WORD OF GOD

The message of the cross is foolishness to those who are perishing, but to us who are being saved it is the power of God. For it is written: "I will destroy the wisdom of the wise, and the learning of the learned I will set aside" (1 Cor 1:18-19).

PERSONAL APPLICATION

In Paul's time, Greek philosophy was flourishing and was looked upon as the highest attainment of Greek culture. In some ways Greeks became intoxicated with learning and were blinded in their pursuit of the beautiful and the good.

How crude and how shocking to these Greek minds did the message of Paul seem! To them, it was unthinkable that God, who is good, beautiful, and happy, would ever descend to become human. Even more shocking was the thought that a god would ever accept death on a cross, a revolting instrument of torture reserved by Romans for non-Roman criminals and run-away slaves. In some ways then, the learning of the Greeks made the Christian message seem foolish.

Although our faith sees God's love for us in the cross, not everyone can accept this. Today we live in a world where we rub shoulders with Buddhists, atheists, Jews, and agnostics. Sometimes we may be hesitant or ashamed to claim our faith as Christians or even to make a sign of the cross in a restaurant. We need to reclaim the cross as *the* central Christian symbol, the source of our power and wisdom.

Reflective Questions:

1) Does my home environment reflect the fact that it is the home of a Christian?
2) Am I willing to be viewed as foolish because of my belief in a crucified Savior?

Suggested Action:

Spend a minute or two looking at the image of Jesus on the cross. Ponder what he might say to you.

MINISTRY OF PRAYER

That the world may see the wisdom of God in the cross of Jesus . . . Lord, hear my prayer.

That, by venerating the cross on Good Friday, we might deepen our faith . . . Lord, hear my prayer.

That we might create a more Christian environment in our work place and our home . . . Lord, hear my prayer.

That I may feel the strength and comfort of the cross when I lie on my death bed . . . Lord, hear my prayer.

CONCLUDING PRAYER

Lord, if the cross is foolishness in the eyes of the worldly, let it ever be a sign of wisdom in my eyes. You alone took an instrument of death and made it a symbol of love. May the cross protect me from the darkness of evil and lead me to eternal light, in the name of the Father, Son, and Holy Spirit. Amen.

(In conclusion, you are invited to take up the cross and kiss it.)

SATURDAY IN SECOND WEEK OF LENT

A cross should be visible and may be used to sign oneself as follows: In the name of the Father, Son, and Holy Spirit. Amen.

OPENING ANTIPHON

I adore you, O Christ, and I praise you because by your holy cross you have redeemed the world.

THE CROSS AND BAPTISM
WORD OF GOD

Are you unaware that we who were baptized into Christ Jesus were baptized into his death? We were indeed buried with him through baptism into death, so that, just as Christ was raised from the dead by the glory of the Father, we too might live in newness of life (Rom 6:3-5).

PERSONAL APPLICATION

Paul tells us that baptism is a direct entrance into the life and grace that comes to us through the death and resurrection of Jesus. It is through baptism that we become children of God, sharers in his life and grace.

In the first centuries, the symbolism of baptism—death and new life—was more clearly seen because the adult convert stepped into a tomb-like bath and disappeared under the water, only to reappear in a few seconds. Water represents the destruction of the old self and the rising to new life as a son/daughter of God. The current practice of pouring water on a baby's head does not express the mystery as effectively as immersion did.

The sign of the cross on the forehead at baptism signifies that the cross is the source of all sacramental life and that baptism is the gateway to the rest of the sacraments. Thus, we walk in the shadow of the cross from the day of our baptism until the day of our final anointing at the moment of our death.

Each day of our lives, we receive from the cross the power to live a Christ-centered life. We may want to escape this responsibility, ignore it, resist it, but baptism marks us forever as children of God.

Reflective Questions:

1) When I make the sign of the cross with holy water, am I reminded of the power of my baptism?
2) Have I claimed the graces and responsibilities bestowed on me at baptism?

Suggested Action:

Attend a baptism or take out mementos of your own baptism and reflect on the meaning of those mementos.

MINISTRY OF PRAYER

For all who will be baptized at the Easter Vigil Service . . . Lord, hear my prayer.

That the Church might be renewed through the Rite of Christian Initiation of Adults (RCIA) . . . Lord, hear my prayer.

For a greater appreciation of our role in the Church through baptism . . . Lord, hear my prayer.

For a greater understanding of my baptismal promises as I renew them on Easter . . . Lord, hear my prayer.

CONCLUDING PRAYER

Creator God, you have marked me as your own from all eternity. As the Church's minister signs the child at baptism, so too, he signs the body in the funeral ritual. The powerful sign of the cross accompanies me throughout my life as I journey from birth to death. May I be ever mindful of the blessings of the cross. Amen.

(In conclusion, you are invited to take up the cross and kiss it.)

THIRD SUNDAY OF LENT

A cross should be visible and may be used to sign oneself as follows: In the name of the Father, Son, and Holy Spirit. Amen.

OPENING ANTIPHON

Through his suffering my servant shall justify many, and their guilt he shall bear.

THE CROSS AND SIN
WORD OF GOD

He was pierced for our offenses, crushed for our sins, upon him was the chastisement that makes us whole, by his stripes we were healed (Isa 53:5).

PERSONAL APPLICATION

Although, in the passage quoted above, Isaiah is probably referring to Israel, the Church has always applied this text and similar texts to Jesus, who represents "the suffering servant." As a suffering servant, Christ willingly shed his blood "on behalf of many *for the forgiveness of sins*" (Matt 26:26-28).

45

Luke describes the crucifixion scene on Golgotha: "It was now about noon and darkness came over the whole land" (Luke 23:44). The Evangelist, far from giving a weather report, was describing the darkness of sin that symbolically enveloped Jesus.

In that dark moment of history, the sins of humanity were represented: murder, jealousy by the Jewish leaders, betrayal by Judas, ambition in Pilate, cruelty by the soldiers, and sacrilegious ridicule. Jesus accepted all of humanity's cruelty to humanity and became a lamb sacrificed for the sins of all. The crucifixion was the epitome of sin.

Through our sins, we were all present at Golgotha. It wasn't just the Roman soldiers who crucified Jesus; people in every age, through their sins, have helped put Jesus on the cross. The song "Were You There?" asks a poignant question. The only answer from a Christian is, "Yes, I *was* there." The human tendency, from Adam on, is to downplay personal responsibility and find scapegoats. The greatest sin in our modern age has been to deny that sin exists. Rather than judging other people, we should humbly say with St. Philip Neri who commented about some prisoners: "There but for the grace of God, go I."

Reflective Questions:

1) Can I imagine Jesus' agony in the garden as he accepted the sinfulness of the whole world (Luke 22:39-46)?
2) Jesus, trusting in his Father, faced the mystery of the other side. If I reflected on my moment of death, would I be able to trust my loving Father?

Suggested Action:

Celebrate the sacrament of reconciliation sometime during Lent, and seek peace with all those about you.

MINISTRY OF PRAYER

For all those who have endured the violence of war and civil unrest . . . Lord, hear my prayer.

For all who know the cross through torture in prison . . . Lord, hear my prayer.

For people who suffer crucifixion through rape, spouse abuse, or child abuse . . . Lord, hear my prayer.

For the grace to accept my own sinfulness . . . Lord, hear my prayer.

CONCLUDING PRAYER

Jesus, the cross has come to be recognized as a sign of your love. During the actual crucifixion, however, the cross represented the barbarous and inhuman treatment of one human being by others. Let me never underestimate the destructive power of sin, so evident in the Good Friday drama, nor minimize the power of your cross to save me. Amen.

(In conclusion, you are invited to take up the cross and kiss it.)

MONDAY IN THIRD WEEK OF LENT

A cross should be visible and may be used to sign oneself as follows: In the name of the Father, Son, and Holy Spirit. Amen.

OPENING ANTIPHON

Christ had to suffer and rise from the dead, and so enter into his glory.

THE CROSS AND JUSTICE
WORD OF GOD

This, rather, is the fasting that I wish: releasing those bound unjustly, untying the thongs of the yoke; setting free the oppressed, breaking every yoke; sharing your bread with the hungry, sheltering the oppressed and the homeless; clothing the naked when you see them, and not turning your back on your own (Isa 58:6-7).

PERSONAL APPLICATION

The Old Testament prophets were always reminding Israel that Yahweh desired justice even before sacrifice and works of religion.

It is obvious that injustice abounds in every age, including that of Jesus. Jesus, in his public ministry, reminded Jewish leaders of the priority of justice. He had nothing but sharp criticism for those who found legal ways to evade their obligation to support their parents (Mark 7:8-13). Likewise, he rebuked those who took the meager savings of widows.

In the case of Jesus' trial, it is clear that he was treated unjustly. Pilate, fearful of another Jewish disturbance being reported to Rome, was more concerned about appeasing the crowds than about treating Jesus with fairness. Pilate's condemnation of the sinless one was the height of injustice.

The words of Isaiah, the prophet, are at the heart of Jesus' teaching. Those words of long ago need to come alive in the Church of this age also. If we are Jesus' disciples, we are compelled by the sign of the cross to work for a just society. Indifference to racial injustice, blindness to poverty, deafness to the cries of the weak and oppressed are modern-day sins as real as the sins of those who nailed Jesus to the cross.

Reflective Questions:

1) How do I see "social justice" as an integral part of the Gospel?
2) Am I satisfied doing charitable works while ignoring the need to also work for a just system?

Suggested Action:

Write a senator/representative about a just cause you believe in, or search out social concern issues in your own neighborhood or parish.

MINISTRY OF PRAYER

For labor and management, that they strive for a balance of justice . . . Lord, hear my prayer.

That nations observe international law in times of peace and war . . . Lord, hear my prayer.

For Church leaders, that they become committed to give just wages to their employees . . . Lord, hear my prayer.

That I learn to listen to the cries of the oppressed in my own neighborhood and society . . . Lord, hear my prayer.

CONCLUDING PRAYER

O Just God, you challenge me to act justly, to love tenderly, and to walk humbly with you. In walking the path of justice, give me the strength to accept the cross of opposition and ridicule which often accompanies that journey. Amen.

(In conclusion, you are invited to take up the cross and kiss it.)

TUESDAY IN THIRD WEEK OF LENT

A cross should be visible and may be used to sign oneself as follows: In the name of the Father, Son, and Holy Spirit. Amen.

OPENING ANTIPHON

I adore you, O Christ, and I praise you because by your holy cross you have redeemed the world.

THE CROSS AND DIVINITY
WORD OF GOD

When the centurion who stood facing him saw how he breathed his last, he said, "Truly this man was the Son of God!" (Mark 15:39).

PERSONAL APPLICATION

One of the first to recognize Jesus' divinity was a pagan centurion. This hard-bitten leader of soldiers had seen many criminals die, but none had died like this man. Instead of cursing people, Jesus held his peace. Instead of condemning people, he forgave them. The centurion, awed by Christ's courage, peace and dignity in the midst of horrible suffering, discovered the Son of God.

The Pharisees taunted Jesus, claiming they would believe in his divinity if he would come down from the cross. In the beginning of his ministry, when tempted by Satan, Jesus had refused to test God by turning stones into bread or jumping from the wall of the temple. Likewise, Jesus reprimanded the Jewish leaders who wanted "signs and wonders," that is, showy miracles.

We, too, often desire extraordinary signs from God; however, in seeking the spectacular we may be blind to the countless ordinary miracles that surround us: the birth of a child, the blossoming of a flower, the rehabilitation of a drug addict, the reconciliation of enemies.

The miracle of Christ's unsurpassable love on the cross is a greater sign of his divinity than any other miracle. We can meditate before the crucifix and, like the centurion, say, "Truly this man was the Son of God!"

Reflective Questions:

1) Is the Good News found in Scripture sufficient for my faith, or do I need extraordinary miracles?
2) Where do I discover the divine breaking through into my ordinary daily living?

Suggested Action:

During the Consecration of the Mass, make an act of faith by saying, "You are the Son of God!"

MINISTRY OF PRAYER

For the unbelievers who cannot see divinity in a god who died on the cross . . . Lord, hear my prayer.

That we might discover God in the patience and courage of those who suffer . . . Lord, hear my prayer.

That we may understand the great miracle involved in a forgiving heart . . . Lord, hear my prayer.

For the grace to see you in my moments of joy and suffering . . . Lord, hear my prayer.

CONCLUDING PRAYER

O Divine Master, at times I want an all-powerful god who will destroy my enemies rather than one who forgives them. Thank you for your amazing grace which allows sinners like me to be saved. May I see your divinity, not so much in "signs and wonders," but in your love on the cross. Amen.

(In conclusion, you are invited to take up the cross and kiss it.)

WEDNESDAY IN THIRD WEEK OF LENT

A cross should be visible and may be used to sign oneself as follows: In the name of the Father, Son, and Holy Spirit. Amen.

OPENING ANTIPHON

Dying you destroyed our death, rising you restored our life. Lord Jesus, come in glory.

THE CROSS AND PAIN
WORD OF GOD

Now I rejoice in my sufferings for your sake, and in my flesh I am filling up what is lacking in the afflictions of Christ . . . (Col 1:24).

51

PERSONAL APPLICATION

At times passages such as the one above by Paul are misinterpreted and Christians are accused of seeking pain for its own sake. But nothing in Jesus' life indicates that he sought pain. In fact, he was accused of the very opposite, of seeking pleasure in food and drink. They said, "Look, he is a glutton and a drunkard . . . " (Matt 11:19).

Certainly such accusations were false, but they did indicate that Jesus, unlike John the Baptist, was no stern ascetic. Both the leisure time Jesus spent at the home of Martha and Mary and his banquets with sinners show him as fully alive and capable of human enjoyments.

Throughout history, especially in the Middle Ages, a certain spirituality has existed which holds in suspicion anything considered painless or too enjoyable. In more modern language, this is termed, "No pain, no gain."

A balanced Christian spirituality does not create pain or enjoy pain; rather it does all in its power to relieve pain. The use of pain killers in hospitals is not merely a humane way to act but also a Christian practice. Pain is not an end in itself; it is nature's way of calling attention to another problem. For example, abdominal pain may indicate an inflamed appendix. If we must suffer pain (and there are times when this is inevitable), then Christ's immense love for each one of us gives added meaning to our pain. He suffered for love of us and assures us he will never be far from us in our pain.

Reflective Questions:

1) What is my pattern of dealing with pain?
2) Have I found comfort in seeing or holding the crucifix during times of pain?

Suggested Action:

If possible, visit someone in pain and try to comfort him/her.

MINISTRY OF PRAYER

For doctors and nurses who minister in cancer clinics or in hospice settings . . . Lord, hear my prayer.

For people who suffer from the pain of war, especially children . . . Lord, hear my prayer.

For those who experience the numbing pain of hunger . . . Lord, hear my prayer.

For the grace to endure the pain I cannot alleviate . . . Lord, hear my prayer.

CONCLUDING PRAYER

Lord Jesus, you came to us in order to heal the wounds of sin and to heal our ills. Divine Physician, lessen my pain, but when there is no easy remedy, enable me to unite my pain with that which you endured on the cross. Amen.

(In conclusion, you are invited to take up the cross and kiss it.)

THURSDAY IN THIRD WEEK OF LENT

A cross should be visible and may be used to sign oneself as follows: In the name of the Father, Son, and Holy Spirit. Amen.

OPENING ANTIPHON

Lord, by your cross and resurrection you have set us free. You are the Savior of the world.

THE CROSS AND AGING
WORD OF GOD

My son, take care of your father when he is old . . . Even if his mind fails, be considerate with him. . . . With your whole heart honor your father; your mother's birthpangs forget not. Remember, of these parents you were born; what can you give them for all they gave you? (Sir 3:12-13; 7:27-28).

PERSONAL APPLICATION

In this passage Sirach reminds us of our debt of gratitude toward our parents. Sirach holds up the virtues of reverence, respect, and gratitude for those who have given us life. These virtues are not readily found in today's society. Although aging is natural, the trend today is to segregate the infirm and aged in nursing homes rather than caring for them within the family circle.

Crosses accompany every stage of our life cycle, and aging is no exception. Indeed, as it is commonly said: "Aging is not for sissies." Sirach points out one of the burdens of old age—loss of memory. He could have also mentioned loss of mobility, diminished hearing or sight, waning energy. In effect, elderly people gradually become more dependent on others, especially their families. That can indeed be humbling.

If we buy into the American consumer premise that "Only what is useful is good," then there is no room for "useless," nonproductive elderly. Our faith teaches just the opposite. All stages of life deserve reverence and respect. God does not love us less when we are aged, and even the most "useless" person is precious in God's eyes.

The spiritual needs of the elderly are of utmost importance. Bringing communion to the homebound, personal visitation, services for the anointing of the sick are beautiful ways for the elderly to experience the love of the parish family.

The faithful are unceasingly challenged to support elderly people in bearing their cross of aging, even to the point of seeking corrective legislation to alleviate the poverty and abuse imposed on many of them.

Reflective Questions:

1) What does the phrase "to age gracefully" mean to me?
2) What elderly person has been a source of inspiration to me? Why?

Suggested Action:

Visit an elderly person who is confined and isolated. Listen carefully to what is being said and reflect on the wisdom you hear.

MINISTRY OF PRAYER

For our aging parents or family members, especially the immobile . . . Lord, hear my prayer.

For the many people who bear the cross of aging . . . Lord, hear my prayer.

For elderly people who are poor and must struggle to meet medical costs . . . Lord, hear my prayer.

That I may accept my own signs of aging . . . Lord, hear my prayer.

CONCLUDING PRAYER

Eternal God, give me the wisdom to respect life at every stage, from birth to death. May I learn to empathize more and more with the infirmities of aged persons. As I grow older, enable me to accept the losses I experience. Help me to remain humble as I become increasingly dependent on the strength and service of others. Amen.

(In conclusion, you are invited to take up the cross and kiss it.)

FRIDAY IN THIRD WEEK OF LENT

A cross should be visible and may be used to sign oneself as follows: In the name of the Father, Son, and Holy Spirit. Amen.

OPENING ANTIPHON

Christ became obedient for us even to death, dying on the cross.

THE CROSS AND SUFFERING
WORD OF GOD

Beloved, do not be surprised that a trial by fire is occurring among you, as if something strange were happening to you. But rejoice to the extent that you share in the sufferings of Christ, so that when his glory is revealed you may also rejoice exultantly (1 Pet 4:12-13).

PERSONAL APPLICATION

In the Old Testament, suffering was often considered a curse, a sign of sinfulness. A dramatic example of this is found in the Book of Job where Job's friends insisted that he must have sinned since he lost everything: his wealth, his health, his family. How could such a curse become a joy?

Peter exhorts the early Christians to rejoice in their sufferings. They needn't seek out suffering for the sake of suffering—that would be masochistic. However, suffering is part of the human condition and, as Peter warns, is part of being a follower of Christ. For Christians, daily suffering must be united with the sufferings of Christ. No suffering in this world goes to waste if we join it to Christ's suffering on the cross.

By his healing power, Jesus relieved the suffering of sickness whenever he could. Yet Jesus obviously did not eliminate all sickness, death, or suffering since he and his apostles were persecuted, suffered, and died. His own mother was no stranger to suffering.

The uniqueness of Christianity is that our suffering takes on new meaning through the cross. "If only we suffer with him [Christ] so that we may also be glorified with him," as Paul reminded the Romans (8:17).

The ultimate answer to the question of why suffering exists will be found in the coming of the kingdom when all tears will be wiped away. In effect, a Christian who shares Christ's cross in this world will share Christ's glory in the next.

Reflective Questions:

1) Suffering enters our lives because we are vulnerable and sinful. What is my attitude when faced with suffering?
2) Where do I experience crosses/suffering in my life?

Suggested Action:

Begin your day by offering it, with all its trials, to Christ crucified.

MINISTRY OF PRAYER

For the conversion of those who inflict suffering on others . . . Lord, hear my prayer.

For innocent victims of war and natural disaster . . . Lord, hear my prayer.

For people who suffer from rare incurable diseases . . . Lord, hear my prayer.

For my friend, _____ , who is suffering and whom I dearly love . . . Lord, hear my prayer.

CONCLUDING PRAYER

Loving Lord, at those times when I feel most abandoned in my suffering, let me experience your presence. As shepherd and guide, lead me through the valley of darkness in order to arrive at the mountain of glory. Amen.

(In conclusion, you are invited to take up the cross and kiss it.)

SATURDAY IN THIRD WEEK OF LENT

A cross should be visible and may be used to sign oneself as follows: In the name of the Father, Son, and Holy Spirit. Amen.

OPENING ANTIPHON

Through his suffering, my servant shall justify many, and their guilt he shall bear.

THE CROSS AND PEACE
WORD OF GOD

For in him all the fullness was pleased to dwell, and through him to reconcile all things for him, making peace by the blood of his cross . . . (Col 1:19-20).

PERSONAL APPLICATION

God the Father's plan, in sending his Son, was to establish a kingdom of peace, based on justice and love. At the birth of Jesus, the angelic choir proclaimed his mission: peace on earth. Jesus brought peace to the world by dying on the cross, thus reconciling us all with God. Before the coming of Jesus, we were estranged from God; but through the cross, we were redeemed and became daughters and sons of God. Moreover, this reconciliation wasn't limited to God's chosen people, the Jews, but it was extended to all humankind.

How strange to associate the cross with peace! Instruments of torture—nails, cross, whip, sword—usually speak more of violence and hatred.

Christ's cross was meant not only to bring peace between God and us but also peace among all nations. Global peace today may seem like an impossible goal, but so did the dismantling of the Berlin Wall. The power of the cross is alive in our world. It's a power to reconcile and forgive. It's a power grounded in prayer.

The peacemaker's role is an ordinary but difficult task, and it begins by taking that first step mentioned in a familiar hymn: "Let there be peace on earth and let it begin with me." However, peacemaking doesn't end with the individual. Supporting or being involved in peace efforts like Pax Christi and Bread For The World are significant ways to bring about global peace.

Reflective Questions:

1) When I feel powerless in working for peace, how do I maintain hope?
2) In what ways do I see myself as a peacemaker?

Suggested Action:

Read John's Gospel on Jesus' gift of peace (John 20:19-23), and thank God for the peace in your life this day.

MINISTRY OF PRAYER

That world governments may seek peaceful solutions to conflict of interests . . . Lord, hear my prayer.

For civil peace among those divided because of religion or ethnic cultures . . . Lord, hear my prayer.

That Christ's peace may reside in our Church and in our families . . . Lord, hear my prayer.

That I may grow in the inner peace that comes from a good conscience and self-respect . . . Lord, hear my prayer.

CONCLUDING PRAYER

Lord, in the midst of a strife-filled world, your peace comes when a right order is restored within myself, among nations, and in all creation. Strengthen your life within me so that your vision of peace will lead me to treat all people and all God's creation with respect and love. Amen.

(In conclusion, you are invited to take up the cross and kiss it.)

FOURTH SUNDAY OF LENT

A cross should be visible and may be used to sign oneself as follows: In the name of the Father, Son, and Holy Spirit. Amen.

OPENING ANTIPHON

Blessed be the Lord day after day, the God who saves us and bears our burdens.

THE CROSS AND PATIENCE
WORD OF GOD

Be patient, therefore, . . . until the coming of the Lord. See how the farmer waits for the precious fruit of the earth, being patient with it until it receives the early and late rains (Jas 5:7).

PERSONAL APPLICATION

In the Old Testament, Job stands out as a classic example of patience. In the New Testament, the disciple James points to

59

the farmer who must wait for his crops to appear. And, in the fourth century, St. Monica prayed for years for her wayward son, until her motherly patience finally bore fruit in the conversion of St. Augustine.

But God is the perfect model of patience. Like the father in the story of the prodigal son, God waits for us to come to our senses after we sin, to seek forgiveness. When Jesus suffered the taunts of the crowd and the ridicule of the soldiers, he modeled the infinite patience of God.

Like our English word "compassion," "patience" is derived from the Latin root "pati," meaning "to suffer." Patience doesn't mean that we bear wrongs which we could change; it means we bear trials and situations which we cannot alter. Webster defines patience as "bearing pains or trials calmly." What a difficult task that is, especially in our modern, instant pleasure-oriented society. How contradictory the prayer: "Lord, give me patience, and give it to me *right now.*"

Job, the farmer, the father, and Monica all experienced the painful cross of waiting—letting go of control and letting God be God. We, too, need patience at work and in the home, with our spouses, our friends, our neighbors, and, yes, with ourselves.

Reflective Questions:

1) Given the fast pace of our modern society, how could I turn occasions of *waiting* into occasions of prayer?
2) What situation is a source of "pain" for me and calls for my patience?

Suggested Action:

Impatience with yourself is often a sign of trying to be too perfect. The next time you feel impatient with yourself, relax and laugh at yourself.

MINISTRY OF PRAYER

For patience as the Church undergoes the difficulties of change after Vatican II . . . Lord, hear my prayer.

For a greater understanding of the weaknesses of other people . . . Lord, hear my prayer.

That adults encourage young people rather than be critical of them . . . Lord, hear my prayer.

That I might accept the inevitable signs of aging . . . Lord, hear my prayer.

CONCLUDING PRAYER

Lord, I, too, can bear fruit when I am patient. Your power brings forth results I could never imagine. Let me be patient with the weaknesses of others and accept my own limitations. May I bear the cross of waiting while I hold fast to the hope of resurrection. Amen.

(In conclusion, you are invited to take up the cross and kiss it.)

MONDAY IN FOURTH WEEK OF LENT

A cross should be visible and may be used to sign oneself as follows: In the name of the Father, Son, and Holy Spirit. Amen.

OPENING ANTIPHON

Blessed be the Lord day after day, the God who saves us and bears our burdens.

THE CROSS AND ABANDONMENT
WORD OF GOD

And at three o'clock Jesus cried out in a loud voice, "Eloi, Eloi lema sabachthani?" which is translated, "My God, my God, why have you forsaken me?" (Mark 15:34).

PERSONAL APPLICATION

How was it possible that the Son of God could feel abandoned by his Father? Scholars have shed some light on this passage by indicating that these words represent Jesus in prayer, and are the opening words of Psalm 22. The ending of that psalm expresses trust in God, and it is most likely that Jesus prayed the entire psalm. It is thought that his words may have expressed a sense of desolation caused by both physical pain and the reality of his approaching death. At this moment in the passion, Jesus, in his humanity, may truly not have felt his Father's loving presence. Yet with naked faith and trust in his Father's love for him and our wounded world, Jesus holds on with an act of the will.

So, too, we who suffer pain and face death may feel some of the same emotions. In our darker moments, we may feel alone and abandoned. Family and friends can accompany us only so far in our journey toward death. Then Jesus, who shares our burdens, will keep his promise to be near us in our suffering and death to give comfort and courage.

There may be occasions when we feel abandoned by God himself. In such times, we must cling to our faith and walk through the darkness. Like Jesus on the cross, such moments of abandonment may demand a sheer act of the will to hold on.

Reflective Questions:

1) When have I felt abandoned by God? What helped me move beyond my feelings?
2) How can I let people minister to me in my times of darkness?

Suggested Action:

Read all of Psalm 22 and connect it with your own life journey.

MINISTRY OF PRAYER

That persons considering suicide may discover reasons to live . . . Lord, hear my prayer.

For children suffering from physical or emotional abandonment by their parents . . . Lord, hear my prayer.

For hostages and those people unjustly sentenced as political prisoners . . . Lord, hear my prayer.

For the times I feel alone, bereft of friends, even God . . . Lord, hear my prayer.

CONCLUDING PRAYER

Lord of Consolation, as you lay in the tomb, you may have seemed abandoned, but your Father was only waiting to give you new life, "Alleluia" life. In my times of darkness, enable me to believe that the cross will lead to a new and glorious life. Amen!

(In conclusion, you are invited to take up the cross and kiss it.)

TUESDAY IN FOURTH WEEK OF LENT

A cross should be visible and may be used to sign oneself as follows: In the name of the Father, Son, and Holy Spirit. Amen.

OPENING ANTIPHON

God did not spare his son, but gave him up to suffer for our sake.

THE CROSS AND SATAN
WORD OF GOD

Now is the time of judgment on this world; now the ruler of this world will be driven out. And when I am lifted up from the earth, I will draw everyone to myself (John 12:31-32).

PERSONAL APPLICATION

In the Old Testament, Satan is viewed as an opponent of God's plan and appears (without being named) as a serpent in the

Garden of Eden. Likewise, Satan tries to thwart God's design by destroying Jesus. In chapter thirteen of John's Gospel, it is recorded that after Judas took a morsel of bread, Satan entered him, and immediately afterwards Judas went out to betray Jesus.

Jesus called Satan the ruler of this world. However, as Jesus moved to his final hour, he knew that the cross would destroy the power of evil and Satan would rule the world no longer.

With the resurrection of Jesus, Satan was defeated once and for all, and Jesus became king of the world. This, however, doesn't mean the power of evil is banished, nor that Satan no longer has influence in this world. The appearance of satanic cults attests to that. It does mean that evil no longer controls the destiny of this world.

The way that Jesus destroyed Satan's power was through love, forgiveness, and sacrifice—all the values represented by the cross. Our weapons against evil remain the same: not hatred but love; not violence but forgiveness; not selfishness but sacrifice.

Reflective Questions:

1) Am I quick to blame Satan for some calamity when human weakness could easily account for it?
2) Sacramentals and the crucifix may be used to counteract the influence of Satan. Does the practice have any meaning for me?

Suggested Action:

Read chapter 12:7-12 of Revelation (Apocalypse) for a partial summary of biblical teaching about Satan.

MINISTRY OF PRAYER

For persons who have experimented with satanic cults, that they may soon divorce themselves from their influence . . . Lord, hear my prayer.

That young people may recognize the dangers of involvement with drugs and cults . . . Lord, hear my prayer.

That the Church's sacramentals may be viewed as symbols of Christ's victorious power . . . Lord, hear my prayer.

That I may experience the wisdom of Jesus' proclamation that the truth will set me free . . . Lord, hear my prayer.

CONCLUDING PRAYER

Creator God, in your plan of salvation, your Son, Jesus, conquered Satan by his death on the cross. May I always put my trust in the power of Jesus, by whose name I am saved. Together with all creation, I will praise his name forever and ever. Amen.

(In conclusion, you are invited to take up the cross and kiss it.)

✝

WEDNESDAY IN FOURTH WEEK OF LENT

A cross should be visible and may be used to sign oneself as follows: In the name of the Father, Son, and Holy Spirit. Amen.

OPENING ANTIPHON

Through his suffering, my servant shall justify many, and their guilt he shall bear.

THE CROSS AND THE GOSPEL
WORD OF GOD

When I came to you . . . proclaiming the mystery of God, I did not come with sublimity of words or of wisdom. For I resolved to know nothing while I was with you except Jesus Christ, and him crucified (1 Cor 2:1-2).

PERSONAL APPLICATION

The newly founded Church in Corinth presented Paul with numerous difficulties. The greatest one was that the Church was divided into several camps. Among the divisions was one group which interpreted Christianity as a "wisdom" religion that was destined for the elite. It tended to identify salvation as some form of exclusive revelation. Not so with Paul who cuts his message down to one unadorned truth: salvation comes through "Jesus Christ and him crucified."

Gospel literally means "good news." In Paul's day, as in our day, the danger is that this good news is not preached or becomes distorted by leaders. The good news is that God the Father so loved us that he sent his Son, Jesus, who suffered and died on the cross for us.

So often we think that salvation has to be earned and thus is the direct result of our good works. How far from the truth that is! God loved us first and salvation is his free gift of love. God is not a petty, vengeful god, but rather a Father who loves us despite our weaknesses.

The comforting message is that we will not be judged on our riches or vast wisdom, but only on our will to love God and our neighbor. The cross that hangs in a Christian home reminds us of the simplicity of the Gospel message, and it urges us to cast aside pride and fear.

Reflective Questions:

1) What is good about the good news of the Gospel?
2) How would I explain the good news to an unbeliever?

Suggested Action:

Reflect on the good news of hope that Jesus gives to the people of Nazareth by reading Luke 4:16-21.

MINISTRY OF PRAYER

That the Church may remain a bearer of good news to the oppressed, the sorrowful, the hopeless . . . Lord, hear my prayer.

For those who preach, that their basic message always echo back to the Gospel . . . Lord, hear my prayer.

That Christian Churches might reflect the good news as they cooperate and seek greater unity . . . Lord, hear my prayer.

That I might live the Gospel with a joyful, grateful heart . . . Lord, hear my prayer.

CONCLUDING PRAYER

Jesus, you came to be a *messenger* of the good news, but you ended up *being* the good news of the Father. On your cross you loved me unconditionally, and you continue to intercede for me in my needs. Help me to believe that you love me, regardless of the times I have doubted or been unfaithful. Amen.

(In conclusion, you are invited to take up the cross and kiss it.)

THURSDAY IN FOURTH WEEK OF LENT

A cross should be visible and may be used to sign oneself as follows: In the name of the Father, Son, and Holy Spirit. Amen.

OPENING ANTIPHON

Christ had to suffer and rise from the dead, and so enter into his glory.

THE CROSS AND GOD'S PLAN
WORD OF GOD

Rather we speak God's wisdom, mysterious, hidden, which God predetermined before the ages for our glory, and which none of the rulers of this age knew, for if they had known it, they would not have crucified the Lord of glory (1 Cor 2:7-8).

PERSONAL APPLICATION

From the very beginning of earth's creation, Satan must have tried to discover God's master plan for it. Likewise, from the very beginning of Jesus' ministry, to the time of his death, Satan suspected that Jesus had a major role in that plan.

The evangelists indicate that Satan, in his efforts to frustrate God's plan, became involved in the betrayal and crucifixion of Jesus. Satan thought that the crucifixion would thwart God's plan,

67

whereas the very opposite was true. To Satan and the blind leaders of the world, God's plan, as Paul says, remained "hidden and mysterious."

That plan for the world has now been revealed through Jesus. However, what about each one of us? How are we part of that master plan? As we move through the stages of our lives, God's plan for us evolves ever so gradually. As we continue to pray and seek God's will, all things will work together for those who love him, even when we sin. *Our Christian life is not determined by fate but by the providence of a loving God.* Paul affirms that God wants to save us and that the crosses we experience in our lives will be a source of salvation.

Reflective Questions:

1) "God's ways are surprising and not our ways." What does this statement mean to me?
2) Was there a time in my life when a heavy cross turned out to be a blessing?

Suggested Action:

Look at your life and see where God has led you providentially. Give thanks to God for the times he has protected you physically and spiritually.

MINISTRY OF PRAYER

That God's kingdom in this world may finally be realized . . . Lord, hear my prayer.

That the Church not lose hope in God's plan in the midst of our confused, troubled world . . . Lord, hear my prayer.

That parents and teachers might reveal God's plan and love for us . . . Lord, hear my prayer.

That I may be able to bend my will and mind to God, whose wisdom is infinite . . . Lord, hear my prayer.

CONCLUDING PRAYER

Lord, your ways are so beyond my comprehension. So often I want to understand why there is suffering and confusion in the world; why there are traumatic changes in society and my life. When there are no answers to my questions, I must trust in your wise providence, O Lord; that all things work for good for those who love you and are called according to your purpose. Amen.

(In conclusion, you are invited to take up the cross and kiss it.)

✝

FRIDAY IN FOURTH WEEK OF LENT

A cross should be visible and may be used to sign oneself as follows: In the name of the Father, Son, and Holy Spirit. Amen.

OPENING ANTIPHON

I adore you, O Christ, and I praise you because by your holy cross you have redeemed the world.

THE CROSS AND PROPHECY
WORD OF GOD

Jerusalem, Jerusalem, you who kill the prophets and stone those sent to you, how many times I yearned to gather your children together, as a hen gathers her young under her wings, but you were unwilling! (Matt 23:37).

PERSONAL APPLICATION

The prophets were called by God to fulfill a mission: to speak strong words of truth or judgment for God. It is no wonder that prophets in any age have been unpopular and often put to death because they faithfully carried out their mission. John the Baptist, Jesus' cousin, fearlessly spoke out in God's name and suffered the same fate as earlier prophets. The crowds, who saw Jesus' miracles and heard his straightforward and courageous message, were soon calling him a prophet.

69

Jesus loved Jerusalem, the Holy City, and in tender poetic language, expressed his desire to shelter his people by gathering them under his wings. But it was not to be! Jerusalem would be "abandoned and desolate" (Matt 23:38). Jesus was sent by the Father, not only to bring a message, but to *be* the message—the Word of God Incarnate. And, for claiming to be God, he was put to death on the cross.

Our challenge is to discern who are the modern-day prophets. Does their message reflect Gospel values? Do their words take flesh in their life-style? Does the prophet remain within the community when he or she faces opposition?

Prophetic words are still spoken in the marketplace and churches throughout our world, but the prophets are often silenced or ignored. Being a critic of the "isms" in our society (e.g., racism, sexism, consumerism), protesting against injustices, confronting the system, whether in government or Church, is truly carrying the cross.

Reflective Questions:

1) Where do I perceive injustice and hear God calling me to take a prophetic stand?
2) What present day Christians would I consider to be prophets—people who speak for God to the Church and society?

Suggested Action:

Become aware of some person whose life/work is prophetic and affirm him/her.

MINISTRY OF PRAYER

That the Church reject what Pope John XXIII called the "prophets of doom" . . . Lord, hear my prayer.

That prophets continue to speak out courageously despite the cross of persecution . . . Lord, hear my prayer.

For those who are prophetic voices in South America and South Africa . . . Lord, hear my prayer.

That I may be open to the prophetic voices of modern times . . . Lord, hear my prayer.

70

CONCLUDING PRAYER

Lord, by my baptism, I, too, am challenged to be a prophet. Yet you send special prophets to the Church and the world to remind me of forgotten Gospel values or to chide me for my sinfulness. Let me not be quick to persecute those who hold the unpopular views, lest I reject the prophets sent by you. Amen.

(In conclusion, you are invited to take up the cross and kiss it.)

✝

SATURDAY IN FOURTH WEEK OF LENT

A cross should be visible and may be used to sign oneself as follows: In the name of the Father, Son, and Holy Spirit. Amen.

OPENING ANTIPHON

Christ has died, Christ is risen, Christ will come again.

THE CROSS AND SICKNESS
WORD OF GOD

When it was evening, they brought him many who were possessed by demons, and he drove out the spirits by a word and cured all the sick, to fulfill what had been said by Isaiah the prophet: "He took away our infirmities and bore our diseases" (Matt 8:16-17).

PERSONAL APPLICATION

There is no indication in the Gospel that Jesus told people to accept their sickness. On the contrary, Jesus attacked disease relentlessly, whenever he encountered it. So the stance of Jesus is that we are called to do all we can to eliminate disease and ill health. As Christians, we welcome the advances of modern

71

medicine and the confirmed miracles of healing at Lourdes, France and elsewhere as gifts of a compassionate God.

When Jesus spoke of taking up the cross, he was in large measure referring to the cross of misunderstanding and persecution. Only later was the meaning of the cross extended to include the acceptance of sickness in its various forms.

Some illnesses result from our own abuse of our bodies, e.g., overeating, excessive smoking and drug abuse. However, there are many illnesses for which we are not directly responsible: sickness due to genes, or to environment (pollution, herbicide), or to the aging process (hardening of the arteries, cataracts). To bear patiently any illness, especially when the illness is not our fault, is to participate in the suffering of the cross. Often, after having tried in vain to be cured by medical means or by faith, we must learn to live with the infirmity as best we can, supported by our faith and the loving care of others. Then Jesus will help us to bear our infirmities, whether of mind or body.

Reflective Questions:

1) Do I have a positive attitude toward my own personal health?
2) Modern medicine and faith healing should be complementary. Where in society do I find positive examples of this?

Suggested Action:

Be good to yourself today. Do something that will refresh your body and spirit.

MINISTRY OF PRAYER

That the Church become a place of healing ministries . . . Lord, hear my prayer.

That the sacrament of anointing of the sick be renewed in the Church . . . Lord, hear my prayer.

That modern science continue its medical research to combat disease . . . Lord, hear my prayer.

That God may lead me to my own ministry of healing . . . Lord, hear my prayer.

God of compassion, you sent your Son to bear our infirmities and diseases. Through his dying on the cross, Jesus gave his promise of ultimate healing. Grant that, through medicine and a strong faith, our modern world may lessen sickness until that final judgment day when there will be no more infirmity. Amen.

(In conclusion, you are invited to take up the cross and kiss it.)

FIFTH SUNDAY OF LENT

A cross should be visible and may be used to sign oneself as follows: In the name of the Father, Son, and Holy Spirit. Amen.

OPENING ANTIPHON

Dying you destroyed our death, rising you restored our life. Lord Jesus, come in glory.

THE CROSS AND THE BROKEN-HEARTED
WORD OF GOD

Blessed are you who are now weeping, for you will laugh (Luke 6:21).

PERSONAL APPLICATION

Truly Mary can be called "The Mother of Sorrows." Who could have been more broken-hearted than Mary on seeing her only Son, Jesus, hanging on a cross? Long before, in the temple, the aged Simeon had predicted that a sword of sorrow would pierce her heart. How right he was!

The crucifixion, so evil and cruel, was the result of the dark side of human nature. Only faith would allow Mary to trust in God and believe that good would triumph. She would cling to that faith like a climber clinging to the face of a mountain.

However, in addition to faith, Mary had her friends. Salome, Magdalen, and the beloved disciple wept with her and consoled her. Luke records Jesus' comforting promise that those who weep will eventually experience joy. Yes, at the resurrection, Mary's bitter tears will become tears of joy.

Nothing tests faith more than the death of a loved one, especially in times of tragic death. We feel empty and broken-hearted. Then, like Mary under the cross, we need the support of others as we wait for the day we will be reunited with our loved ones and experience unending joy.

In today's Church, responsibility for the "ministry of consolation" belongs, not only to priests, but to the total community. The healing process for the broken-hearted takes time and needs the consolation of loving friends as well as the balm of the Holy Spirit.

Reflective Questions:

1) How have I been a healing presence for a person grieving someone's death?
2) As I recall those who ministered to me when I was broken-hearted, what did they do or say that was especially helpful?

Suggested Action:

If there is bereavement ministry in the parish, ask how you might help. If not, maybe you could be the one to initiate that ministry.

MINISTRY OF PRAYER

For those who are missing in action in recent times . . . Lord, hear my prayer.

That more people in the Church might accept the call to be ministers of consolation . . . Lord, hear my prayer.

For parents who have lost young children in Sudden Infant Death Syndrome or other tragic ways . . . Lord, hear my prayer.

That my own painful experience of loss might enable me to comfort others . . . Lord, hear my prayer.

CONCLUDING PRAYER

Consoling God, Mary suffered a broken heart from the crucifixion of her Son. When a cross threatens to crush me or snuff out the fragile flame of hope, strengthen my faith and trust in you. Let my heart experience healing so that I may become more understanding of and compassionate toward others. Amen.

(In conclusion, you are invited to take up the cross and kiss it.)

MONDAY IN FIFTH WEEK OF LENT

A cross should be visible and may be used to sign oneself as follows: In the name of the Father, Son, and Holy Spirit. Amen.

OPENING ANTIPHON

Dying you destroyed our death, rising you restored our life. Lord Jesus, come in glory.

THE CROSS AND FORGIVENESS
WORD OF GOD

When they came to the place called the Skull, they crucified him and the criminals there, one on his right, the other on his left. Then Jesus said, "Father, forgive them, they know not what they do" (Luke 23:33-34).

PERSONAL APPLICATION

Forgiveness is at the heart of Jesus' message. How often should we forgive those who injure us? Jesus tells us to forgive them seventy times seven—that is, never stop forgiving. What is even more astounding is this: Jesus refers not only to our family or friends or fellow citizens, but also our enemies, those who ridicule us or hate us.

Jesus practiced what he preached. In his dying hours, he forgave Pilate and the cruel soldiers, the high priest and the Pharisees who mocked him under the cross. In fact, he even pleaded ignorance on their part, as a lawyer would before a judge. Such forgiveness is beyond the human, as our own daily life experience would testify. Love for our enemies remains a genuine sign of the power of grace. Only with the help of God can we truly let go of life's hurts and open our hearts to healing.

Letting go of vengeful and hateful thoughts does not erase the pain inflicted by those who hurt us. On the cross, Jesus felt the pain even though he forgave his enemies. Letting go is but the first brave step in our process of healing.

The Church provides ritual opportunities for forgiveness: at the beginning of the Mass; at the sign of peace; and especially in the sacrament of reconciliation.

When we pray the powerful words of the "Our Father," we make a tough bargain with God, namely, that God will "forgive us our trespasses as we forgive those who trespass against us."

Reflective Questions:

1) What are the hurts and angers within me that I need to let go of?
2) It is easier when another person comes to me for forgiveness. Am I willing to initiate the process of reconciliation with another?

Suggested Action:

Think of someone who has hurt you. In your heart, commend that person to the goodness and loving care of the Lord.

MINISTRY OF PRAYER

That divided Christians in Ireland might seek a peace based on justice . . . Lord, hear my prayer.

That true racial justice be established in South Africa . . .
Lord, hear my prayer.

That different factions within the Catholic Church be more
open to reconciliation . . . Lord, hear my prayer.

That I might be an instrument of peace within my family
. . . Lord, hear my prayer.

CONCLUDING PRAYER

Jesus, as you were dying on the cross, you generously forgave your friends for their infidelity and cowardice and forgave even those who had nailed you there. Grant that I may imitate your example, and let me not nurse my hurts and wounds, nor hold onto a grudge or a hateful anger, but strengthen my will to let go and forgive. Amen.

(In conclusion, you are invited to take up the cross and kiss it.)

TUESDAY IN FIFTH WEEK OF LENT

A cross should be visible and may be used to sign oneself as follows: In the name of the Father, Son, and Holy Spirit. Amen.

OPENING ANTIPHON

Lord, by your cross and resurrection you have set us free. You are the Savior of the world.

THE CROSS AND COMPASSION
WORD OF GOD

For we do not have a high priest who is unable to sympathize with our weaknesses, but one who has similarly been tested in every way, yet without sin (Heb 4:15).

PERSONAL APPLICATION

Jesus' compassion made him strikingly different from the rabbis of his day. Not only was he moved with pity for the sick, but he also was moved to action: he healed them. And because Jesus didn't hesitate to cure people on the Sabbath, an action his critics considered forbidden by the law, his compassion often resulted in hostile relations with the Pharisees.

Christ's compassion extended beyond the physically or mentally ill to the spiritually ill. Jesus was known as a friend of sinners, a man who ate with them and visited their homes. When Jewish leaders brought to him a woman caught in adultery, Jesus shamed away the leaders but allowed the woman to leave with only the reminder to sin no more. Even on the cross Jesus was compassionate, turning to a repentant thief and assuring him of paradise. Such compassion attracted sinners to repent, and it has continued to touch people down the centuries.

The struggle to carry our cross can make us compassionate persons. When we have suffered, we understand not only our own weaknesses but also the weaknesses of others. It is as a wounded healer that a widow can best reach out to another widow or a divorced person can best minister to another divorced person. It is in such outreach that the Church continues Christ's ministry of compassion.

Reflective Questions:

1) Am I quick to judge others before trying to walk in their shoes?
2) Are there wounds in me that haven't been healed and which block my compassion to others?

Suggested Action:

Listen with your heart to one who is suffering, and try to empathize with him/her.

MINISTRY OF PRAYER

That the Church, first and foremost, become a haven of compassion . . . Lord, hear my prayer.

That pastoral ministers of care reach out to the suffering in nursing homes and hospitals . . . Lord, hear my prayer.

That through ministry to persons with AIDS, the Church might be a sign of healing . . . Lord, hear my prayer.

That I may continue to grow in compassion and resist pharisaical self-righteousness . . . Lord, hear my prayer.

CONCLUDING PRAYER

Jesus, you who are the good shepherd know my weaknesses well. Comfort me with your healing touch and patiently search for me when I stray from your love. As you heal my wounds, open my heart to minister to others in your name. Amen.

(In conclusion, you are invited to take up the cross and kiss it.)

WEDNESDAY IN FIFTH WEEK OF LENT

A cross should be visible and may be used to sign oneself as follows: In the name of the Father, Son, and Holy Spirit. Amen.

OPENING ANTIPHON

Christ became obedient for us even to death, dying on the cross.

THE CROSS AND HEALING
WORD OF GOD

And just as Moses lifted up the serpent in the desert, so must the Son of Man be lifted up, so that everyone who believes in him may have eternal life (John 3:14-15).

PERSONAL APPLICATION

In this passage, John is referring to an incident recorded in Numbers 21:4-9. Because of their murmuring, the Israelites were punished by God, who allowed deadly serpents to bite them. In order to be healed, the Israelites had to gaze upon a serpent image which Moses had erected on a pole.

John says that in a similar manner, those who look on Jesus crucified and believe in him will have eternal life. Just as it was faith in the power of Yahweh that healed the Jews, so it is faith in Jesus Christ that will heal us ultimately—in heaven.

The beginning of all healing is "love': love of self, love of others, and love of God. Without this right order, we can never be totally healed. Holistic healing implies a harmony within us, a peaceful union of mind, heart, and body. Thus ulcers may be alleviated by medicine, but a person who cannot let go of deep-seated angers and self-hatred may never know complete healing.

The cross can be healing if it leads us to experience the deep love of God for us. In 1807, while still a young man, Blessed Eugene De Mazenod (founder of the Oblates of Mary Immaculate), had a profound experience of Christ's personal love when he saw the cross unveiled at a Good Friday service. That Good Friday awakening changed the course of his life, and eventually he founded a missionary society that preached the good news of the cross. Like Blessed Eugene, we, too, may be moved by Christ's love on the cross to find new meaning in life and see God's gentle hand guiding us.

Reflective Questions:

1) Have I ever had a personal awakening while contemplating the crucifix?
2) Do I experience dis-ease in my heart? Reflect on the possible reasons for any unrest.

Suggested Action:

Consider giving a crucifix as a gift to someone on some special occasion, e.g., his/her birthday or wedding.

MINISTRY OF PRAYER

That the cross be a central symbol in our homes . . . Lord, hear my prayer.

That the cross recover its real "sign" value of God's personal love . . . Lord, hear my prayer.

That the veneration of the cross on Good Friday be an occasion of healing for many . . . Lord, hear my prayer.

That the cross remind me during Lent of my need for spiritual health . . . Lord, hear my prayer.

CONCLUDING PRAYER

Healer God, you know well the brokenness in my life. The image of your Son, broken on the cross, can heal me with the medicine of love. May I endeavor to love myself as I love my neighbor and God. Open my heart to experience the power of the cross as I struggle to put my life in right order. Amen.

(In conclusion, you are invited to take up the cross and kiss it.)

THURSDAY IN FIFTH WEEK OF LENT

A cross should be visible and may be used to sign oneself as follows: In the name of the Father, Son, and Holy Spirit. Amen.

OPENING ANTIPHON

Those who sow in tears shall reap with shouts of joy.

THE CROSS AND PERSECUTION
WORD OF GOD

Beloved, do not be surprised that a trial by fire is occurring among you, as if something strange were happening to you. But rejoice to the extent that you share in the sufferings of Christ, so that when his glory is revealed, you may also rejoice exultantly (1 Pet 4:12-13).

PERSONAL APPLICATION

Persecution, referred to by Peter as "trial by fire," was not unusual for Christians of Peter's time. For him, when Christians were persecuted for Christ's sake or for his Gospel, it was a cause for rejoicing. No doubt Peter recalled the beatitude proclaimed by Jesus: "Blessed are they who are persecuted for the sake of righteousness, for theirs is the kingdom of heaven" (Matt 5:10).

Jesus said that if enemies of the truth have persecuted him, they will persecute his disciples as well. Persecution of Christians has continued down through the ages as one manifestation of the continuous war being waged against God's plan by the powers of evil.

Sometimes Christians are persecuted for being followers of Christ, as happened during the Roman persecutions. Sometimes, sadly enough, Christians even persecuted each other, as during the Middle Ages. In our day, Christians have been persecuted for upholding Gospel ideals of social justice, as has occurred in El Salvador, where Archbishop Romero was killed.

In what way do we encounter persecution because of our values? Are we treated unfairly because we are elderly or because of our sex, color, or religion? Are we ridiculed because of our "pro-life" or "anti-war" stance? It is not easy to rejoice in this kind of suffering, but Peter puts before us this ideal: "no cross, no glory."

Reflective Questions:

1) I can recall a particular time when I felt persecuted. How did I react?
2) If I never take a stand on anything, I may be compromising the Gospel. Is there an area of injustice where I could effect change, but haven't acted?

Suggested Action:

By word or deed support a person you feel is being treated unjustly.

MINISTRY OF PRAYER

For the countries that still limit freedom of worship . . . Lord, hear my prayer.

For Christians who suffer in the marketplace because of their moral values . . . Lord, hear my prayer.

For followers of Christ who are ridiculed or suffer prejudice because of their religious beliefs . . . Lord, hear my prayer.

That I might have the courage to name injustice when I see it and work for change . . . Lord, hear my prayer.

CONCLUDING PRAYER

Defender of the oppressed, I have not always lived your Gospel of peace, love and service. Yet I have discovered that when I try to live according to the Gospel, your strength empowers me, despite my timidity. Give me the courage to proclaim your message in the face of ridicule. Amen.

(In conclusion, you are invited to take up the cross and kiss it.)

FRIDAY IN FIFTH WEEK OF LENT

A cross should be visible and may be used to sign oneself as follows: In the name of the Father, Son, and Holy Spirit. Amen.

OPENING ANTIPHON

Blessed be the Lord day after day, the God who saves us and bears our burdens.

THE CROSS AND FAITH
WORD OF GOD

And he [Peter] said to him, "Lord, I am prepared to go to prison and to die for you." But he replied, "I tell you, Peter, before the cock crows this day, you will deny three times that you know me" (Luke 22:33-34).

PERSONAL APPLICATION

For the followers of Christ, the darkest moments of faith came at the time of his arrest and crucifixion. Scripture tells us that during the passion one apostle betrayed Jesus and another denied knowing him. The other apostles fled, probably hastening towards the friendly territory of Galilee. Only a few women, one male disciple, and Jesus' mother were present under the cross.

Jesus was very understanding of the fear and weakness his apostles faced when confronting the cross—even of a Judas who took his own life. In a post-resurrection meeting with Peter along the beautiful shores of the Sea of Galilee, Jesus forgave him. Peter's three-fold denial was erased by a three-fold declaration of love for Jesus.

When everything in our lives is going along smoothly, it is easy to follow Christ. But it is in times of trial and suffering that our faith is tested and grows strong. How very difficult it is to see the hand of God in times of divorce, death of a loved one, depression, or illness. The temptation might be to resort to anger, denial, or despair. If we accept these crosses and hold fast, trial and adversity can help our faith grow strong in areas where it has been weak. Only faith in Jesus Christ will enable us to walk through our garden of Gethsemane.

Reflective Questions:

1) When did I encounter someone who had become embittered through adversity?
2) What is my greatest fear or worry? Do I try each day to turn it over to God?

Suggested Action:

Reflect on a cross God has given you. Make an act of faith and surrender yourself to God's care.

MINISTRY OF PRAYER

For people who are tempted to deny Jesus or his teachings . . . Lord, hear my prayer.

For Christians besieged with serious doubts of faith, that God may give them blessed assurance . . . Lord, hear my prayer.

For people who are maliciously misunderstood, that they may be forgiving . . . Lord, hear my prayer.

That God may strengthen my faith as I face my personal garden of Gethsemane . . . Lord, hear my prayer.

CONCLUDING PRAYER

Christ, my rock of strength, during times of doubt and despair, be the foundation of my life. If you are on my side, Jesus, who can be against me? As I struggle with the trials of each day, encourage me by your loving care. Amen.

(In conclusion, you are invited to take up the cross and kiss it.)

SATURDAY IN FIFTH WEEK OF LENT

A cross should be visible and may be used to sign oneself as follows: In the name of the Father, Son, and Holy Spirit. Amen.

OPENING ANTIPHON

God did not spare his Son, but gave him up to suffer for our sake.

THE CROSS AND SCANDAL
WORD OF GOD

For Jews demand signs and Greeks look for wisdom, but we proclaim Christ crucified, a stumbling block to Jews and foolishness to Gentiles . . . (1 Cor 1:22-23).

PERSONAL APPLICATION

What signs did the Jews demand of Jesus? One sign they wanted is recorded in the passion: ". . . if you are the Son of God, come down from the cross!" (Matt 27:40). If Jesus had performed this miracle, they supposedly would have believed.

A scandal can cause a lapse of faith or at least be a test for one's faith. For the Jewish leaders, the cross was a scandal or a stumbling block. Why was the cross seen as a scandal by the Jewish leaders? In Deuteronomy it is written that ". . . God's curse rests on him who hangs on a tree . . ." (21:23). Thus a crucified person was considered cursed. Surely Yahweh would not allow the true Messiah to come under a divine curse through crucifixion. They concluded that Jesus could not be the Messiah.

Although the Jewish leaders disbelieved, thousands of Jews overcame the stumbling block and were baptized on Pentecost. For Judas, the cross was a scandal; for the Roman centurion, it was a source of salvation. Such is the paradox of the cross.

Faith in a crucified Christ is a gift. For those who believe, no explanation of the cross will be demanded; for those who don't, no explanation will suffice.

The danger today is to seek a cushioned cross, one that makes no demands and asks no sacrifices. In our zeal to win converts, we can never water down the core message of the Gospel. The cross will forever be a sign of contradiction, touching the hearts of some and repulsing the hearts of others.

Reflective Questions:

1) How would I explain Jesus' death on the cross to a little child?
2) When have I felt repulsed by the cross?

Suggested Action:

Take a moment to give thanks for the gift of your faith in Christ crucified.

MINISTRY OF PRAYER

That the Jews, God's chosen people, may find salvation . . . Lord, hear my prayer.

For a change of heart in Christians who bear prejudice towards Jews . . . Lord, hear my prayer.

For a better dialogue among Jews, Christians, and Moslems . . . Lord, hear my prayer.

That my faith may be strong enough to withstand any scandal within the Church . . . Lord, hear my prayer.

CONCLUDING PRAYER

Crucified Christ, you have taken an instrument of torture and punishment and made it a symbol of grace and mercy. The cross continues to touch the uneducated and the scholar; saint and sinner; patriot and criminal. I pray that the cross never be a stumbling block for me but rather a sign of your immense love. Amen.

(In conclusion, you are invited to take up the cross and kiss it.)

PALM SUNDAY

A cross should be visible and may be used to sign oneself as follows: In the name of the Father, Son, and Holy Spirit. Amen.

OPENING ANTIPHON

Praise to our King, the Son of David, the Redeemer of the world; praise to the Savior whose coming has been foretold by the prophets.

THE CROSS AND TRIUMPH
WORD OF GOD

On the next day, when the great crowd that had come to the feast heard that Jesus was coming to Jerusalem, they took palm branches and went out to meet him, and cried out: "Hosanna! Blessed is he who comes in the name of the Lord, (even) the king of Israel" (John 12:12-13).

PERSONAL APPLICATION

On the surface, it seems that Jesus was never closer to becoming a king than at the moment of his entry into Jerusalem. Previously, after the miracle of fishes and loaves, the crowd had wanted to proclaim Jesus as their King, but he had fled back to the mountains alone.

Now, in great triumph, he entered Jerusalem, the city he loved. Ironically, in a short time the crowds (perhaps some of the same people) would be asking for his crucifixion. Jesus knew that he could not shrink from the hardening opposition of the Jewish leaders nor trust the acclaim of the fickle crowds. This entry into Jerusalem played a major part in his destiny.

Even in what seemed to be a show of worldly triumph, Jesus almost humorously had the last word. Instead of choosing a white Arabian steed, as a military leader would, Jesus came riding on an ass. He knew that his destiny was to die on a cross in Jerusalem. His Father's will held sway over any desire for popularity.

In our American society, people are often judged by what they own or wear or what they do. Our society has its heroes in sports, music, film, or politics. Passing honors, popularity, prestige are often just that—PASSING. Here today and gone tomorrow. Our success story, like that of Jesus, is in doing God's will each day, even if his will leads us to the cross.

Reflective Questions:

1) Have fame and popularity ever betrayed me? If so, how?
2) As morality in our country becomes based on surveys and opinion polls, how might I be influenced by such polls?

Suggested Action:

Place a piece of blessed palm next to the cross and reflect on the fleeting nature of fame.

MINISTRY OF PRAYER

That Christians prepare themselves well for the sacred mysteries of Holy Week . . . Lord, hear my prayer.

That our governments realize that death and destruction result from war . . . Lord, hear my prayer.

That the Palm Sunday procession might remind Christians to give loyalty to Christ . . . Lord, hear my prayer.

For the wisdom to realize the folly of basing my life on fame and popularity . . . Lord, hear my prayer.

CONCLUDING PRAYER

Christ, Redeemer King, you understood the emptiness of worldly fame, and power. For you, doing the will of the Father was the litmus test of any action. Let me not place my trust in money, fame, or power, but in the simple humble truth of the Gospel. Amen.

(In conclusion, you are invited to take up the cross and kiss it.)

✝

MONDAY IN HOLY WEEK

A cross should be visible and may be used to sign oneself as follows: In the name of the Father, Son, and Holy Spirit. Amen.

OPENING ANTIPHON

I have the power to lay down my life and I have the power to take it up again.

THE CROSS AND OBEDIENCE
WORD OF GOD

After withdrawing about a stone's throw from them and kneeling, he prayed, saying, "Father, if you are willing, take this cup away from me; still, not my will but yours be done" (Luke 22:41-42).

PERSONAL APPLICATION

Jesus did not accept death on the cross with an easy nod of the head. As a sensitive human being, he understood only too well the horror of the cross. In his short lifetime, he may have even seen someone hanging on a cross. It was in the Garden of Gethsemane that Jesus, envisioning the suffering ahead of him, wrestled with obedience to his Father's will—wrestled until he sweat blood. In Hebrews (5:8) it is written, "Son though he was, he learned obedience from what he suffered. . . . "

Just as in the garden the first Adam committed the sin of disobedience, it was in another garden that Jesus, the second Adam, made an act of obedience. That act of obedience was so powerful that Jesus brought salvation to the world and became the model for his followers, even to this day. Jesus, by saying "Yes" to his Father's will, became our Lord and Redeemer.

It is often difficult to know the will of God. Sometimes God uses other people (e.g., spiritual directors), events, our conscience, and even our crosses, to reveal his will. However, at times, we must enter our own garden of Gethsemane and wrestle with God's will—wrestling not only to discover it but also to obey it. Although we may sin or stray because of our weakness or blindness, God, as a jealous lover, will await our return.

Reflective Questions:

1) What roadblocks get in the way of my hearing God's voice?
2) When have I found that obedience to lawful authority might be in conflict with my inner obedience to God?

Suggested Action:

Pray the "Our Father" slowly, allowing the words to sink into your heart.

MINISTRY OF PRAYER

That our spiritual leaders may be obedient to God's will . . . Lord, hear my prayer.

That the United Nations seek peace and justice according to God's design . . . Lord, hear my prayer.

For people facing difficult moral dilemmas, that they may seek God's will in prayer . . . Lord, hear my prayer.

That I cultivate the habit of praying to God before making important decisions . . . Lord, hear my prayer.

CONCLUDING PRAYER

Loving Father, in wisdom you gave your Son, Jesus, to the world as the model of living, loving, and obeying. Like Jesus, I too must learn through the crosses of my life how to obey you. When I face important decisions, teach me to pray for guidance, and strengthen me when I too must say, "Not my will but yours be done." Amen.

(In conclusion, you are invited to take up the cross and kiss it.)

✝

TUESDAY IN HOLY WEEK

A cross should be visible and may be used to sign oneself as follows: In the name of the Father, Son, and Holy Spirit. Amen.

OPENING ANTIPHON

Jesus, meek and humble of heart, make my heart like unto yours.

THE CROSS AND HUMILITY
WORD OF GOD

Who, though he was in the form of God, did not regard equality with God something to be grasped at. Rather, he emptied himself, taking the form of a slave . . . he humbled himself, becoming obedient to death, even death on a cross (Phil 2:6-8).

PERSONAL APPLICATION

Although Jesus was equal to God and worthy of praise and glory, the striking characteristic of his life was his humility. He was never proud, arrogant, vain, or demanding of privilege. Born in a manger, nailed to a cross like a slave, and buried in a stranger's tomb, Jesus taught us to learn of him, meek and humble of heart.

Jesus' humility was manifested best when he served others. In his life he ministered to the lowly: to the poor and powerless, to sinners, to women and children. What a startling act it must have been for Jesus, the Master, to wash the feet of his disciples before sharing the Last Supper with them. St. Augustine said that "Wherever humility is, there is also charity." A truly humble person like Jesus will look to the interests of others.

Jesus discovered, however, that people can be selfish and demanding and that service to them can become a real cross. The multitudes pressed in on him, complained and made demands on him. The crowd that he fed once wanted to be fed again and again. Yet Jesus never gave up on them.

Through the insights of psychology, Christians of our age have become aware of the many forms of false humility. We no longer think of humility as utter self-abasement, denying who we are. We need to claim our God-given gifts and talents and put them at the service of others. In doing so, we will discover the cross in the heavy expectations of people. As a consequence, prolonged service to others will demand generosity, perseverance and humility.

Reflective Questions:

1) What person in my family or neighborhood comes to mind when I think of humility?
2) Do I honestly claim my talents and use them to serve others?

Suggested Action:

Do some thoughtful service for another, knowing that there may be no recognition or affirmation in response.

MINISTRY OF PRAYER

For deacons, in their ministry of service to others . . . Lord, hear my prayer.

For women religious who, by giving of themselves, have been an example of generosity . . . Lord, hear my prayer.

That the Church may always reach out to the poor and the powerless . . . Lord, hear my prayer.

That I might examine my motives for service to others . . . Lord, hear my prayer.

CONCLUDING PRAYER

Creator God, your Son came as a helpless infant born of a humble maiden, Mary. He proclaimed glad tidings to the poor, liberty to the captive, and tirelessly served the crowds. Enable me to imitate the humility of Jesus and to serve others selflessly as he did. Amen.

(In conclusion, you are invited to take up the cross and kiss it.)

WEDNESDAY IN HOLY WEEK

A cross should be visible and may be used to sign oneself as follows: In the name of the Father, Son, and Holy Spirit. Amen.

OPENING ANTIPHON

Jesus Christ loved us, and poured out his own blood for us to wash away our sins.

THE CROSS AND LOVE
WORD OF GOD

. . . I live by faith in the Son of God who has loved me and given himself up for me (Gal 2:20).

PERSONAL APPLICATION

In this one sentence, Paul sums up the love story of Jesus Christ, who went to the limits for each one of us. What makes God's love different, what makes the love of Jesus unique, is that he died for sinners. Paul admits that a good person might reluctantly die for another just person, but God proved his love by dying for us while we were still sinners (Rom 5:7-8). The real scandal and glory of the cross is the unconditional love of God for prodigal humankind. God does not love us because of our goodness or intelligence, our wit or attractiveness. Rather God has loved us first because he has chosen to, and his love is an outrageous transforming love.

Human love is far more than an emotion. At its best, it is unselfish and caring; yet it has its limitations. Jesus challenges us to love our enemies, something that is beyond the capability of merely human love.

Jesus exhorts us to love as he did, but such love doesn't happen overnight. Ideally this generous love is modeled for us within our family setting and beyond, to our neighborhood and community. Realistically, this generous love is challenged by those who seem unlovable, obnoxious, or even hateful. Rubbing shoulders with such people is where the cross appears. At times love prompts us to forgive; at other times, to ask to be forgiven.

Reflective Questions:

1) How is God inviting me to find room in my heart for a "difficult" person?
2) How do I view "tough love," allowing people to suffer the consequences of their sins or addictions in order to be healed?

Suggested Action:

Think of some person who dislikes you or even hates you. Keep that individual in your prayers today.

MINISTRY OF PRAYER

For child abusers and their victims, that healing might be realized . . . Lord, hear my prayer.

For victims of crime, that God may help them forgive their assailants . . . Lord, hear my prayer.

That racially prejudiced people may experience a conversion of heart . . . Lord, hear my prayer.

That I might be grateful to those who have blessed me with unselfish love . . . Lord, hear my prayer.

CONCLUDING PRAYER

God of love, I marvel at your generosity towards all, saint or sinner, poor or rich. Daily I struggle with your ideal to love my neighbor, especially when that neighbor is hateful or offensive. Use me as an instrument of your peace and a channel of your love. Amen.

(In conclusion, you are invited to take up the cross and kiss it.)

HOLY THURSDAY

A cross should be visible and may be used to sign oneself as follows: In the name of the Father, Son, and Holy Spirit. Amen.

OPENING ANTIPHON

The Son of Man did not come to be served but to serve, and to give his life as a ransom for many.

THE CROSS AND EUCHARIST
WORD OF GOD

While they were eating, Jesus took bread, said the blessing, broke it, and giving it to his disciples said, "Take and eat; this is my body." Then he took the cup, gave thanks, and gave it to them, saying, "Drink from it, all of you. . . ." (Matt 26:26-27).

PERSONAL APPLICATION

How familiar, yet awesome, are the words and actions of Jesus as he shared the Last Supper with the apostles. They could not fully comprehend that they were sharing in a sacrificial meal wherein the bread and wine would become Jesus' own body and blood. That Jesus would soon die on the cross was a part of the salvation drama yet to unfold. Later the Church would remain true to Jesus' command: "Do this in memory of me."

The Church teaches that each time the priest, Christ's representative, celebrates Eucharist, that same sacrifice of Calvary is once more present to us. The congregation responds after the consecration by proclaiming: "When we eat this bread and we drink this cup, we proclaim your death until you come."

Worship and service to others are, of necessity, bound together. It was no accident that John's Gospel relates how Jesus washed the feet of the apostles at the Last Supper. After completing the ritual, Jesus said, " . . . as I have done for you, you should do" (John 13:15). By serving others, we strive to imitate Christ by dying to our own selfishness and growing in our love for others. On Holy Thursday the Church invites us to approach the Lord's table with heartfelt gratitude for the gift of Jesus and to renew our pledge of service to others.

Reflective Questions:

1) Has my understanding and appreciation of the Eucharist grown since Vatican II?
2) Where do I sense God calling me to greater service in my parish and community?

Suggested Action:

Attend Holy Thursday Mass if possible, or read about the Last Supper in John's Gospel, chapters 13–15.

MINISTRY OF PRAYER

That on this feast of Holy Thursday, pastors may recommit themselves to serving the needs of their parishioners . . . Lord, hear my prayer.

That Christians recommit themselves to serving others . . .
Lord, hear my prayer.

That the needs of the poor will be especially remembered
in this celebration . . . Lord, hear my prayer.

That I may grow in appreciation of the Eucharist . . . Lord,
hear my prayer.

CONCLUDING PRAYER

Jesus, I am mindful of the gift of the Eucharist that you gave
to the Church. I likewise remember how you humbly washed feet
and asked me to imitate you. Grant me a hunger for your Eucharist
and allow me to be blessed and broken in service to others. Amen.

(In conclusion, you are invited to take up the cross and kiss it.)

✝

GOOD FRIDAY

A cross should be visible and may be used to sign oneself
as follows: In the name of the Father, Son, and Holy Spirit. Amen.

OPENING ANTIPHON

This is the wood of the cross, on which hung the Savior of
the world. Come, let us worship.

THE CROSS AND SACRIFICE
WORD OF GOD

Now since it was preparation day, in order that the bodies
might not remain on the cross on the sabbath, . . . the Jews asked
Pilate that their legs be broken and they be taken down. But when
they came to Jesus and saw that he was already dead, they did
not break his legs . . . For this happened so that the scripture

passage might be fulfilled: "Not a bone of it will be broken" (John 19:31-36).

PERSONAL APPLICATION

The Passover Feast commemorated the liberation of the Hebrews from Egyptian slavery. In the historical account of that liberation, the Israelites placed the blood of the lamb on their door-posts so that they might be saved from the angel of death.

In John's passion account, the death of Jesus takes place at a time when the priests would be slaughtering the lambs for the Passover meal. Since Jews could not bury the dead on the Sabbath, the leaders requested Pilate to hasten the death of the criminals by beating them with iron rods. In the case of Jesus, who was already dead, the soldiers pierced his side *instead* just for an added assurance. In John's theology, Jesus represents the Passover Lamb, the bones of which were *not to be broken*. Just as the blood of the lamb had saved the Israelites from the angel of death, so Jesus, by shedding his blood on the cross, liberated us from sin and death.

What possible meaning could the term "Paschal Lamb" have for Christians today? Jesus wants to free us from the fear of death and the power of sin. He wants us to enjoy the inner freedom of a child of God. The Eucharist is a time to recall our liberation and to praise and thank God for it.

Reflective Questions:

1) What fears in me call out for God's liberation?
2) Has the sacrament of reconciliation been a freeing experience for me?

Suggested Action:

When the veneration of the cross takes place in the Good Friday service, give thanks to God for freeing you.

MINISTRY OF PRAYER

That Jerusalem may remain a holy place and become a city of peace . . . Lord, hear my prayer.

For friends who are carrying the heavy cross of addiction
. . . Lord, hear my prayer.

For all who participate in the Good Friday services, that they appreciate Christ's sacrificial love for them . . . Lord, hear my prayer.

That I find renewed meaning in the ritual signing of the cross . . . Lord, hear my prayer.

CONCLUDING PRAYER

Crucified Savior, through your death on the cross, you gave your life that I might live. By the power of the cross, we have become your people. By your blood, free me from obsessive fears and sins. I ask this in your name. Amen.

(In conclusion, you are invited to take up the cross and kiss it.)

HOLY SATURDAY

A cross should be visible and may be used to sign oneself as follows: In the name of the Father, Son, and Holy Spirit. Amen.

OPENING ANTIPHON

O happy fault, O necessary sin of Adam, which gained for us so great a redeemer!

THE CROSS AND HOPE
WORD OF GOD

Our hope for you is firm, for we know that as you share in the sufferings, you also share in the encouragement (2 Cor 1:7).

PERSONAL APPLICATION

Paul was an amazing person, able to keep hope alive even in the midst of varied trials and tribulations, including shipwreck, stoning, sickness. The secret of his strength was his vibrant virtue of hope. The source of his hope was Jesus Christ.

As Jesus was dying on the cross, aware that he would soon be buried in a tomb, what held his world together? It appeared that all was lost—the kingdom, his dreams, his small band of followers. All that remained was hope based on faith. It was a hope in his Father's power; a hope in new life; a hope in his Father's plan for the world. Jesus held onto the edge of darkness with whitened knuckles as he awaited the hour of his burial, but the darkness of the tomb would give way to the brightness of Easter morn.

The early Church ritually commemorated Christ's passage from death to resurrection, from darkness to light, by keeping vigil. The Church today, in its renewed liturgy, likewise commemorates Jesus' passage from death to life. The Easter Vigil begins with darkness penetrated only by the light of the paschal candle, a symbol of Christ.

Christ told us that we must also be a light to the world. The well-known Christopher motto reminds us, "Better to light one candle than to curse the darkness." We can give up on our wounded world or we can reach out to the abandoned and depressed with a smile, a kind word, or a good deed. The choice is up to us.

Reflective Questions:

   1) When I have experienced periods of darkness, what has kept me going?
   2) What would be my response to a person who despairs of any meaning in life?

Suggested Action:

Read about Paul's difficulties in being an apostle (2 Cor 11:16-29).

MINISTRY OF PRAYER

For all who are bedridden and seek hope in Christ . . . Lord, hear my prayer.

That the Church may minister to families who have experienced tragic loss . . . Lord, hear my prayer.

For political prisoners who feel abandoned . . . Lord, hear my prayer.

That I might never give way to despair, but rather pray for the virtue of hope . . . Lord, hear my prayer.

CONCLUDING PRAYER

Lord, it is so difficult to carry the cross and not lose heart. Open my eyes to see small signs of hope along my way of the cross. Strengthen my faith to see beyond the darkness of this life to the light of Easter glory. Alleluia.

(In conclusion, you are invited to take up the cross and kiss it.)

EASTER SUNDAY

A cross should be visible and may be used to sign oneself as follows: In the name of the Father, Son, and Holy Spirit. Amen.

OPENING ANTIPHON

You have mourned for Christ's suffering: now may you celebrate the joy of his resurrection. Alleluia.

THE CROSS AND VICTORY
WORD OF GOD

Was it not necessary that the Messiah should suffer these things and enter into his glory? (Luke 24:26).

PERSONAL APPLICATION

Someone once suggested that the shortest Easter homily would be, "Satan lost." Not only was Satan conquered, but sin and death likewise. Indeed, the cross, a symbol of torture and death, has now become a sign of victory also. A victory we too can claim.

This symbol of both torture and victory has been portrayed in Christian art over the centuries. In some museums, crosses beautifully designed and adorned with priceless jewels are displayed. These crosses represent the triumphant joy of Christians and stand in marked contrast to the almost ghastly corpus of the suffering Christ found in some cultures. There is room in our tradition for both.

In the history of Christianity, there has been a tendency to emphasize one aspect or the other of the cross. Regardless of emphasis, there is no victorious cross without a suffering cross, no Easter without a Good Friday.

Ultimately, we are assured that the cross God gives us will become a victorious cross. The cross of suffering we bear will someday become the bejeweled cross of victory. We know that no matter what suffering comes our way—it will end. We are commissioned to bear witness to Christ's victory, here on earth. We must be a living alleluia from head to toe. It is said, "If in your heart you believe in the resurrection, let your face show it."

Reflective Questions:

1) How does my faith in the risen Christ enable me to enjoy life?
2) How would I answer people who claim that a crucifix negates the resurrection?

Suggested Action:

Take the cross you have used during Lent and decorate it as a sign of Easter victory.

MINISTRY OF PRAYER

That our churches keep alive the victorious hope and joy of Easter . . . Lord, hear my prayer.

That the Church, undergoing Vatican II changes, may arise stronger and more alive . . . Lord, hear my prayer.

That our faith may lead to a healthy optimism, even when confronted with world crises . . . Lord, hear my prayer.

That my life may be a witness to the fact that my Redeemer lives . . . Lord, hear my prayer.

CONCLUDING PRAYER

Lord and Savior, you have walked with me along this Lenten journey. The Good Friday cross becomes the glorious cross of Easter. Keep an Easter hope and joy alive in my heart each day of my life. As I share in your suffering, let me share also in your glory. Amen. Alleluia! Alleluia! Alleluia!

(In conclusion, you are invited to take up the cross and kiss it.)

Robert Eimer, O.M.I., published his first book, *Tilted Haloes,* in 1964. He has served as pastor in St. Paul and Duluth, Minnesota. Currently he is the pilgrimage director at Our Lady of the Snows Shrine, Belleville, Illinois. He has collaborated with Sarah O'Malley, O.S.B., in authoring *Come Let Us Celebrate* (1986), *In the Potter's Hands* (1988), and *Journey of Decision* (1991).

Sarah O'Malley, O.S.B., has an M.A. in theology from St. John's University, Collegeville, Minnesota. She is the director of ministry of care at St. Thomas the Apostle Parish in Phoenix, Arizona. Her first book, *Age and Grace,* published by The Liturgical Press in 1980, was co-authored with Bill Fournier, O.M.I. With Robert Eimer, O.M.I., she has written, *Come Let Us Celebrate* (1986), *In the Potter's Hands* (1981), and *Journey of Decision* (1991).